Larry Wilde's Complete Book of Ethnic Humor

Larry Wilde's Complete Book of Ethnic Humor

with a Foreword by
George Jessel

Bell Publishing Company
New York

This 1984 edition is published by Bell Publishing Company,
distributed by Crown Publishers, Inc.,
by arrangement with Pinnacle Books, Inc.

This book was originally published as
The Complete Book of Ethnic Humor.

Manufactured in the United States of America

Library of Congress Cataloging in Publication Data

Wilde, Larry.
  Larry Wilde's Complete book of ethnic humor.

  1. Ethnic wit and humor. I. Title. II. Title:
Complete book of ethnic humor.
PN6231.N3W54 1984   818'.5402   84-14626

ISBN: 0-517-45128X

h g f e d c b a

To:
Lloyd Gaynes, Barry Glazer,
Mort Fleischmann, Ernie Medwig,
Sidney Miller, Tony Noice,
Morris Resner, Ned Sukin,
and Stanley Steven Wandermann III.
— the guys who have given me
a lifetime of laughter.

"A hearty laugh relieves me;
and I seem better able after
it to bear my cross."

A. LINCOLN

"And if I laugh at any mortal thing
'Tis that I may not weep."

LORD BYRON

"Forgive, Oh Lord, my little jokes on thee
And I'll forgive thy great big one on me."

ROBERT FROST

"Give me a sense of humor, Lord;
   Give me grace to see a joke.
To get some happiness from life;
   And pass it on to other folk."

LARRY WILDE

CONTENTS

FOREWORD

The Heritage of Ethnic Humor

BY GEORGE JESSEL

THE ability to laugh at oneself or one's family and friends is a great and happy gift. It shows a true comic spirit. But even more it proves that man can survive most tragedies by seeing the funny side of life.

Ethnic humor in America has a strong heritage. It developed from the people themselves and then carried over to the stage. At first, white men blackened their faces and made people laugh. There were MacIntyre and Heath, Moran and Mack, Amos and Andy.

Soon the wonderful black entertainers came on the scene. Williams and Walker, Miller and Lyle and many others who were popular around the turn of the century.

In those days we had fun with Dutch and German comedians. There were Weber and Fields, The Rogers Brothers, Sam Bernard, and Bert Lahr.

Then there were the so-called Yiddish comedians—
Joe Welch, Ben Welch, Honey and Lee, Smith and
Dale, and many others. Vaudeville also had its share of
Italian comics. George Beban, Clark and Verdi. And oh,
yes, there were the great Irish jesters.

These men and their way of making people laugh
has never disappeared from society. Laughing at the
language mistakes and idiosyncracies of grandparents
and relatives from the old country has always been
considered good-natured fun. It's part of America's
great heritage of humor. I'm happy that this book will
be a lasting tribute to ethnic comedy.

ACKNOWLEDGMENTS

No one can accomplish a single feat without help. If you are lucky enough to be surrounded by talented people it makes the accomplishment so much more pleasant. I hereby express deep appreciation to Robin Fields, my speedy typist, Jane Jordan Browne, my assiduous literary agent, and Maryruth Wilde, my beautiful wife.

An extra special note of gratitude goes to Andrew Ettinger, my masterful editor, without whose sense of humor and faith in the project this book could never have been produced.

Larry Wilde's Complete Book of Ethnic Humor

INTRODUCTION

Comedy is a form of dramatic literature designed
to amuse and often to correct or instruct through
ridicule. To achieve its effects, it exposes
incongruity, absurdity, and foolishness, and its
treatment of characters frequently has elements
of exaggeration and caricature.

ENCYCLOPEDIA AMERICANA

"Man," wrote Nietzche, "is the animal most capable
of suffering and he had to invent laughter to preserve
his sanity." Aristophanes, the great Greek writer of
comedy, began poking fun at men and institutions
about 400 B.C. Since then, exploiting life's absurdities
to amuse has become a time-honored diversion.

A number of theories exist about what constitutes

1

comedy. Humor has been classified as being sinister, aggressive, and degrading, as well as uplifting. When the elements of anger and frustration are added to that concept, you have the basic formula for ethnic humor.

As far back as Plato and Aristotle, provoking belly laughs by exposing excess and pomposity has been an accepted part of literature. Through the centuries, great names such as Rabelais, Martial, Shakespeare, Cervantes, Swift, Carroll, Dickens, Twain, and Shaw enriched the tradition. And then, during the nineteenth century in America, a new amusement form began to capture the public's fancy: the minstrel show. This innovative stage presentation was quickly followed by burlesque and vaudeville. Soon silent movies were providing people with the opportunity to snicker at their fellow homo sapiens. Then the miracle of modern electronics came upon the scene—recordings, radio, talking pictures, and television. Suddenly, there was an abundance of comedy and now human beings had a choice of which medium could best titillate their funny bone.

But, through all of man's newly discovered methods of amusement, in spite of these entertainment miracles, one form of communication, one means of personal, immediate contact and reaction among human beings remained. It has stayed the same, albeit refined, throughout the centuries, and that is the gentle art of wisecracking.

The term *wisecracking* is a fairly modern one but its roots can be traced at least as far back as Shakespeare. In *Much Ado About Nothing* the Bard of Avon wrote: "A college of witcrackers cannot flout me out of my humor."

The evolution of the word wisecracking is now explained by Evan Esar in his *The Humor of Humor* (Bramhall House). "Shakespeare had merely extended the application of the word *crack*, which, with *break*, had been used in connection with jests. A witcracker was therefore a person who broke jests or cracked jokes."

2

Wisecracks are usually insults. They are almost always exaggerated witticisms that overstate something about a particular person or thing.

The most popular of all exaggerations is the wisecrack that ridicules the special traits of an individual by means of absurd illustration. And this is the essence of *ethnic* humor.

The *American Heritage Dictionary* defines *ethnic* as a religious, racial, national, or cultural group. The following joke, told around Southern California, exemplifies the true substance of ethnicity in humor, for it encompasses no less than four races and three religious groups.

> Why is Sunday morning the best time to be on the Los Angeles Freeways?
> The Catholics are in church.
> The Protestants are still asleep.
> The Jews are in Palm Springs.
> The Indians are restricted to the reservation.
> The Chinese are stuffing fortune cookies.
> The Blacks are stealing hubcaps.
> And the Mexicans can't get their cars started.

The most popular kind of ethnic joke is the putdown joke, which ridicules specific "character traits" of a particular group. The person telling the joke wants you to believe that these traits are true.

In analyzing the above joke, we see that certain ethnic group characteristics have been exaggerated for comedic purposes. Obviously, *all* Catholics are not in church, as *all* Protestants are not asleep, *all* Jews are not vacationing in Palm Springs, Indians are *not* restricted to the reservation, the Chinese don't stuff fortune cookies, most Blacks are decent law-abiding citizens, and not all Mexicans have cars.

We laugh at the images that the gag created. It conjures up certain recognizable ethnic characteristics. Though these traits are not *true* they *are* familiar and we laugh even though we know that the barbed jest has no basis in truth.

The jokes told about other minorities in America are, again, based on the behavior patterns that are known and generally accepted about that particular group. The French, for example, are considered great lovers of women, wine, and food so they are kidded about those sensual appetites.

We think of the Russians as being totally involved in politics, the Germans being political as well as warlike. Scots and money go hand-in-hand.

If we were to take the eccentricities that are identifiable with specific nationalities and use their quirks and peculiarities to create a humorous situation we would have the following joke:

> A cruise ship, with passengers from all over the world, was caught in a severe storm and wrecked on a remote and unexplored island.
>
> Soon the island began to buzz with activity. The GERMANS were drilling the natives into the Army. The JEWS opened up a department store. The ITALIANS began organizing some hookers and the FRENCH started a restaurant. The SCOTS were financing the whole thing and a couple of ENGLISHMEN were still standing around waiting to be introduced.

THE POLISH JOKE SYNDROME

Why do Polacks wear turtleneck sweaters?
To hide their flea collars.

Did you hear about the Polack who went to visit his girlfriend and found she didn't have very much on?
He went back nine months later and she had a little moron.

What do they call a dance attended by a bunch of Polacks?

A goof ball.

Polish Jokes are the best example of the barbed jest—*best* because there is no such thing as a Polish joke, per se. In Poland, almost all the jokes are political in nature. Poland has been a subjugated country and it is the Poles' way of coping with years of dictatorship and foreign intervention.

In America the very gags that poke fun at Poles are also told about the Irish, Blacks, Puerto Ricans, Mexicans, Gypsies, Swedes, Finns, Arabs, and the Indians. The following *Polish* jokes are also told as *Italian* jokes:

If you see a row of houses that all look alike, how can you tell which one is Italian?

It's the one with the diving board over the cesspool.

Why did the Italian mother decide to have her baby in the drugstore?

Because they had free delivery.

Did you hear about the Italian who stayed up all night studying for his urine test?

In the early 1940's the popular joke craze on college campuses as well as in the war plants was *The Little Moron* jokes. The fad disappeared as soon as World War II ended. They surfaced again in the 1960's, only this time moron jokes were called *Polish* jokes.

It also depends on where you live. Around San Francisco, Polish jokes are called *Portuguese* jokes. In Canada, they are referred to as *Newfie* jokes (after the residents of Newfoundland). In South Dakota, they are *Norwegian* jokes. Texans poke fun at the students of Texas Agricultural and Mechanical University who are, by and large, farmers. So, as far as Texans are concerned, moron jokes or Polish jokes are really *Aggie* jokes.

If that isn't confusing enough, in France, *Scottish* jokes are attributed to the Swiss. In Sweden, moron jokes are told about the residents of Norway. Russians tell Czech jokes. The English tell moron jokes on the Irish.

THE SMILING IRISHMEN

Jokes about Irishmen began to flourish as the first immigrants from the Emerald Isle arrived on our shores in the 1840's. The potato fields in Ireland were black and rotten, and to avoid starvation over two and a half million Irishmen set sail for America.

They were naive—unsophisticated and totally unused to big city life. Before long their country bumpkin characteristics led them to be known as "greenhorns." The following is an example of the kind of moron joke told about the new arrivals:

> Murphy came from an inland Irish town, and on his arrival in New York, found his way to the Battery. For three days he hung around the pier where a gigantic anchor lay on the planks.
>
> "Is there anything I can do for you?" asked a stevedore who noticed Murphy staring at the giant anchor.
>
> "No, thank ya," replied the Irishman. "Oi'm jest waitin' ta see who the man is that can swing that pick!"

Around the turn of the century Irishmen began sending large numbers into three professions: politics, the priesthood, and the police. By escaping the ghettos and entering legitimate, respected work the Irish stepped up the rungs of society; and gags (moron jokes) about Irish ignorance and incompetence faded. Soon they were replaced with quips about councilmen, cops, and Catholics.

The Sons of Erin provided jokesmiths with additional subject material by their reputation for drinking and brawling. However, there is another element of humor that became part of the Irish comic spirit. It has been attributed to Obadiah Bull, an Irish attorney in London during the reign of Henry VII. Lawyer Bull was supposed to have been a notorious blunderer, often making statements that contradicted each other.

Soon other Irishmen got into the habit of making these utterances of paradox, which although appearing to have two opposite meanings turned out to have a logic all their own. They have since come to be known as *Irish Bulls:*

> Policeman: Say, you, if you're gonna smoke here you'll have to either put out your pipe or go somewhere else.

"If they ever drop the bomb on us," said Mrs. Callahan, "they'll blow us all to maternity."
   "Yeah," agreed Mrs. Quinlan, "and we won't know who to blame either."

> Father Fallon: Abstinence is a wonderful thing.
> MacNamara: Sure an' it is, Father, if practiced in moderation.

THERE WILL ALWAYS BE AN ENGLAND

Often Irish humor is mistakenly lumped together with the English, which quickly raises the ire of any true Irishman. There is a lot that is funny about the British. Again, national idiosyncrasies provide the jokemakers with much material.

The *English* have a reputation for being terribly reserved, even standoffish. Their attitude toward sex seems Victorian, yet homosexuality appears to be accepted and practiced rather openly. The British become comically absurd when trying to explain their point of view in their typical superior manner:

Sir Reginald Farthington was on trial before the high court of Australia for the crime of molesting an ostrich.

"Before passing sentence," announced the judge, "do you have anything to say?"

"Your honor," said the Englishman, "if I'd have known you were going to make such a fuss about it, I'd have married the bloody bird!"

THE RED MAN

Did you hear about the Algonquin Chief who named his daughter "ninety-nine cents" because she was always under a buck?

That is the kind of joke Americans find funny about Indians. But what do American Indians laugh at? An example of a favorite joke would be an animal out-witting a human being. Man's foibles are another source of amusement. Indians also have the ability to laugh at themselves. For they, too, have suffered the humiliations of being a minority.

The essence of true Indian humor is almost child-like. It is innocent and simple, unencumbered with subtlety. Pranks are a key source of laughter. If there was such a thing as an Indian stand-up comedian, he would be a prankster not a joketeller. His technique would be visual not verbal.

This approach to comedy stems from the Red Man's background. Indians were divided into nations, tribes, even clans within those tribes. Therefore communication was difficult. Each group had its own language. And so a universal means of communicating developed—sign language—which thus became the instrument for relating humor.

THE FUNNY FAR EAST

The Western world does not understand many things about the mysterious Far Easterners. Their sense of humor is one of them.

There are about 680,000 Japanese-Americans and 610,000 Chinese-Americans in the United States. The Chinese have been here since the 1840's, the Japanese since the 1880's. Although both groups have contributed significantly to our culture in the arts, sciences, politics, and business few examples of the oriental sense of humor can be found in literature.

The word joke in Chinese is literally translated to mean "smile talk." Orientals rarely laugh out loud. They are amused. They smile. However, there are certain idiosyncrasies to poke fun at, in particular the orientals' transposition of the l and r sounds when they speak English:

Did you hear about the new Japanese camera, on the market?
When you trip the shutter, it goes "crick!"

American ethnic humor utilizes racial characteristics, historical facts, and word-play in this joke:

Did you hear about the guy who was half-Japanese and half-black?
Every December 7 he attacked Pearl Bailey.

And ol' Pearlie May brings us to . . .

THE BLACK COMIC SPIRIT

Blacks discovered what Jews had learned thousands of years ago: that humor is the way to reduce tension by attacking whatever threatens us.

9

The black approach to comedy evolved from the days of bondage on the southern plantations. Although immigrants of various ethnic backgrounds found their way here voluntarily, blacks were hijacked from different African nations and sold into slavery.

"Music played a large role in the survival of the black people in America," write Redd Foxx and Norma Miller in their *Encyclopedia of Black Humor* (Ward Ritchie Press). "That . . . and a sense of humor that just couldn't be enslaved."

In the evenings down South after a long day of back-breaking drudgery, the "darkies" would form a semicircle and take turns entertaining. There was singing and dancing and hand clapping, and much merriment. Laughter helped release the pent-up anger and frustration of a life of servitude.

The "nigras" became expert at imitating their master's mannerisms. They poked fun at the white man by mimicking him through impersonations and comic impressions guaranteed to evoke belly laughs. They strutted and pranced and mocked the cockiness of the oppressive plantation owners to the delight of their fellow slaves.

Here is a sample of the kind of humor that provoked guffaws in the 1860's:

A slave owner called Uncle Tom up to the main house. "Ah, dear, faithful, loyal Uncle Tom," cried the Southerner. "Lincoln has forced you to accept freedom, against my wishes, and I am sure, against yours. Dear old friend, and servant, you need not leave this plantation. Stay here with us; kindly, gentle, self-sacrificing Uncle Tom!"

"Thank you, deah, kine lovin', gen'rous Massa," said the newly freed man. "I recken I'll leave. But befo' I go I wants you ter know I will allus 'membuh you ez de son uv a bitch you is an allus wuz!"

Blacks have been snickering at Whitey ever since. Like the Jews, blacks developed a grin-and-bear-it attitude toward their unfortunate predicament. Laughing was a way of coping, and they've been laughing for 300 years. The following joke illustrates the bridge blacks have crossed in humor from slavery to the Seventies:

An N.A.A.C.P. official telephoned the Library of Congress and told the chief librarian that the library had 18,000 books with the word 'nigger' in them and that all the books had to be removed in a week.

"But," protested the librarian, "we have 50,000 volumes with the word 'bastard' in them."

"I know," said the official, "but you bastards aren't organized."

THE JEWISH SENSE OF HUMOR

Jewish jokes are a thing apart. Some are interchangeable with those directed at other minorities, but most stories are indigenous to the Jews.

Actually, Jewish jokes form the foundation for all ethnic humor. One reason is that Jews have been a minority longer than any other group and historically have been used as the butt of biting barbs. Another, and more important, reason is that humor is part and parcel of the Jewish culture.

The Jewish sense of humor has been the guiding light through dark centuries of prejudice and persecution. It has been the pin by which they have pricked the thick bubble of adversity. The "chosen people" have taught themselves to laugh at their enemies. More importantly, they have learned to laugh at themselves.

During the Nazi reign of terror in Germany in the 1930's Jews were taunted, tormented and beaten, and eventually shipped to concentration camps for extermination. And yet, they found it possible to laugh. Imagine, despite the horror and tragedy, the following story was making the rounds:

11

Rabinowitz, hiding with his wife from the Nazis in a secluded Berlin attic, decided to get a breath of fresh air. While out walking he came face to face with Adolph Hitler.

The German leader pulled out a gun and pointed to a pile of horse manure in the street. "All right, Jew!" he shouted, "eat that or I'll kill you!" Trembling, Rabinowitz did as he was ordered.

Hitler began laughing so hard he dropped the weapon. Rabinowitz snatched it up and said, "Now, you eat the manure or I'll shoot!" The Fuhrer got down on his hands and knees and began eating.

While he was occupied, Rabinowitz sneaked away, ran through an alley, climbed over a fence, and dashed up the stairs to the attic. He slammed the door shut, bolted and locked it securely. "Bessie! Bessie!" he shouted to his wife. "Guess who I had lunch with today!"

Lenny Bruce, ahead of his time with his poignant comedic insights, was a student of his craft. Bruce is credited with the humor formula: *Tragedy + Time = Satire.*

This equation is the cornerstone for most Jewish humor. Business failure, family heartbreak, Hitler's holocaust, sorrows of every nature provide subjects that have been joked about by Jews.

This ability to laugh at adversity seems to be the key to Jewish survival. Paradoxically, it has also been the spring that nurtured the development of the "American sense of humor." Much of the comedy as it exists today on the stage, in motion pictures, and television has been created, molded, and delivered by Jewish comedians and comedy writers.

Only because Jews are joke-oriented could the following story have come about. It is the absolute refinement of the Jewish sense of humor:

Morton and Fogel were discussing humor over lunch. "Do Jews react differently when they hear a joke?" asked Morton.

"What a question?" replied Fogel. "If you tell an Englishman a joke he'll laugh at it three times. Once, when you tell it, again when you explain it and third time when he understands the point.

"Tell a German the same joke, he'll laugh twice. Both times to be polite. There won't be a third time, because he'll never get the point.

"Tell the same joke to an American, he will laugh once, immediately, because he'll get it right away."

"But," said Fogel, "when you tell the joke to a Jew . . ."

"Yes?" asked Morton.

"When you tell the same joke to a Jew, he won't laugh at all. Instead, he'll say, 'It's an old joke—and besides, you told it all wrong!"

SEX AND ETHNIC HUMOR

Many of the gags in this collectoin have a spicy flavor. It is common knowledge among comedians that jokes with erotic content evoke the biggest response from an audience. Since sexual mores in America have always been couched in the Puritanical ethic, the mere mention on stage of mating allows the crowd to release whatever frustrations or hang-ups they have about the subject.

The second most powerful comedic weapon for the nightclub comic is the ethnic joke. A story about a dress manufacturer can be funny—tell it about a *Jewish* manufacturer of ladies apparel and you add a dimension that can turn the same story into a scream.

Dress manufacturer is general. A *Jewish* dress manufacturer is precise, exact, pinpointed. An audience can identify more emotionally with specifics. The story becomes funnier when the audience can visualize the person concerned. It is emotion that causes the big laugh. Tell a mother-in-law joke to an unwed college student and he *might* smile. Relate it to a married man who isn't particularly fond of his wife's mother and you get a laugh of recognition, of identification.

An ethnic joke with a sexual connotation has a doublebarreled explosiveness that almost guarantees a sure-fire response.

THE AMERICAN SENSE OF HUMOR

Americans can trace their ancestors to countries all over the world and are proud of the land of their fathers. But now they live in America. In the land of the free. So it is that Poles can laugh at Polish jokes; Jews will scream at Jewish jokes; Irishmen are convulsed by Irish jokes and so on down the line.

The jokes in this book are in actuality representative of the *American* sense of humor. In being able to see what's funny about our fellow man we recognize ourselves. The irony of it all is that when we ridicule the special characteristics of some minorities we are in fact mocking the entire human race. For are we not all plagued with pomposity, prejudice, and false pride?

By lumping together the "character quirks" of several nationalities in one joke we can quickly discover the essence of the American comic spirit:

Put two men and a woman on a desert island and this is what surely will happen.

If they're JEWISH, the two men will play cards to see who gets the woman.

If they're ENGLISH, they'll discuss the weather and ignore the woman because they're more interested in each other.

If they're FRENCH, the two men will share the woman.

If they're ITALIAN, the woman would kill one of the men.

If they're ESKIMOS, one of the men will claim the woman and then lend her to the other man.

If they're AMERICANS, they'd still be discussing the matter, trying to find a fair and amicable way to settle the problem.

As Will Rogers once said, "Everything is funny as long as it is happening to somebody else." Ethnic humor is an integral part of our heritage. It will be with us as long as we are a nation of many peoples from many lands and as long as we are able to laugh at ourselves. Laughter is the tonic that keeps Americans healthy.

AMERICA! A toast to your good health!

LARRY WILDE

AMERICAN INDIAN

A Shawnee chief from a reservation was visiting in Chicago. While wandering around the town he was stopped by a native of the Windy City who asked, "How do you like our town?"

"All right," replied the Chief. "And how do you like our country?"

Markowitz, a New Yorker traveling through New Mexico, stopped at an Indian souvenir depot. He spotted an old Navajo selling blankets.

"How much?" he asked.

"Hundred dollar," said the Indian.

"Nothing doing," said Markowitz.

"How much you give?"

"Twenty-four dollars."

"Listen, wise guy," said the Navajo, "bargains like Manhattan Island you ain't gonna get no more."

Did you read about the New York nightclub just opened by Indians?

They charge you twenty-four dollars for a Manhattan!

To the Earliest Americans, thrift was a virtue. Many an Indian Princess made a hit with the braves because she was tight with a buck.

Peter Minuit had just completed the purchase of Manhattan Island from the Canarsie Tribe and was standing with the sellers on the banks of the East River surveying the purchase. "Say, wait a minute," he exclaimed, "isn't that Brooklyn over there?"

"Listen, wise guy," replied the Canarsie chief, "for twenty-four dollars you expect the place to be perfect?"

An Indian girl was soliciting some business along New York's Park Avenue. When a john asked how much, she replied, "A hundred dollars."

"A hundred dollars!" sputtered the guy. "All of Manhattan only cost twenty-four!"

"That's right, baby," she smiled. "But Manhattan just lies there."

A pretty Powahatan working as a waitress in a roadside restaurant was being annoyed by a two-bit Casanova. He used lines like: "Indian Princess do it for a buck?" and "How about Indian Princess go into forest with white man?"

"Come on, honey," he finally said, "you wanna make whoopee with me? Tell me in Indian."

She looked at him and replied, *"Ugh!"*

Did you hear about the Indian health nut who switched to filtered smoke signals?

Big Eagle and Gray Blanket were camped near the desert in New Mexico. Suddenly there was an A-bomb explosion and a huge mushroom-shaped cloud. Big Eagle turned to his friend, "It's for you—answer it!"

Yellow Feather was standing on a nearby mountain sending up smoke signals. He, too, saw the atomic explosion and as the smoke hurled skyward for miles, he muttered, "Gee, I wish I'd said that!"

Two Mohican scouts, Big Bear and Black Hawk, watched silently from their place of concealment behind some shrubbery as the first white settlers set foot on the North American continent. After quietly studying the scene for several minutes, Black Hawk turned to Big Bear and said, "Well, there goes the neighborhood."

Virgin Squaw: A wouldn't Indian

Did you hear about the Algonquin Chief who named his daughter "Ninety-nine Cents" because she was always under a buck?

While visiting a Blackfoot village in one of the Dakotas, an Army scout rode to the Chief's lodge, where he was to remain for the night. The Blackfoot leader came out and received him while his squaw unsaddled the horse and placed the equipment alongside their teepee.

"Will my things be safe there?" asked the scout.

"Yes," replied the Chief, "there isn't a white man within two days' ride of here."

Then there was the Indian Chief who installed electric lights in the tribal latrine, thus becoming the first Indian to ever wire a head for a reservation.

The Indian agent on a South Dakota reservation reports that the Sioux squaws have been practicing a variation on suburban wife-swapping. They call it "passing the buck."

An Indian Maiden, A Sioux,
As tempting as fresh honeydioux,
   Liked to show off her knees
   As she strolled past teepees
And hear the braves holler, "Wioux-Wioux!"

When the railroads began their westward thrust, one of the companies wanted its tracks to run through Zuni wastelands, and offered the chief of the tribe $10,000 for the property.

"$50,000," said the Zuni leader.

"Why," said the railroad's representative, "that land is hilly, full of rocks and clay; it's no good for farming or anything else."

"Maybe not," said the Chief, "but good for railroad."

On a very hot afternoon Chief Bold Blanket and his wife were traveling across the plains on a rickety old train.

The Chief ordered his squaw to fetch him a drink of water. She waddled down the train corridor and returned shortly with a brimming cup of water.

Drinking it quickly he demanded, "More," and off she went down the swaying corridor. He drank the second and once again demanded, "More."

The squaw again made her trek to the water source only to return promptly with an empty cup.

"Where water?" asked the Chief.

"Paleface sitting on well."

A Seminole looked at a ham sandwich he had just ordered in a restaurant. "You slice 'em ham?" he asked the short order cook.

"Yep," said the man.

"Well," said the Indian, "you damn near miss 'em."

A Cherokee Chief asked an Oklahoma bank for a loan of $300. "What security have you got?" the banker asked him.

"Got 150 horses."

This was satisfactory so the loan was granted.

Several weeks later the Chief came into the bank, pulled out a huge roll of bills, counted off the $300, plus interest due the bank, and started to leave.

"Wait," said the banker, "you've got a lot of money there. Why don't you let us take care of it for you?"

"How many horses you got?" asked the Indian.

Letter received by the Bureau of Indian Affairs:

"Gentlemen:

I've always wanted to have an affair with an Indian. How do I go about it?"

An old Iroquois was standing on top of a hill, with one arm around his young son. As they both gazed down into a beautiful lush valley below them, the Indian said to his boy: "Some day, my son, all this land will belong to the Indians again. Paleface all go to the moon."

In a little New Mexico town, a pretty young tourist overheard a virile Navajo saying "chance" to every passing female. Finally, her curiosity got the best of her and she walked up to him and said "Hello."

To which he answered, "Chance."

"I thought all Indians said 'How'!"

"I know how—just want chance," he replied.

Did you hear about the American Indian couple who are sending their kids to Camp Rabinowitz for the summer?

A Chickasaw Chief's daughter had been away at college. At the end of her Freshman year she returned to the reservation obviously pregnant. She walked into her father's teepee, held up her right hand, and said "How!"

The Chief stared at her swollen stomach. "Me know how," he grunted. "What me want to know is — who?"

Tonto and the Lone Ranger were surrounded by 2,000 bloodthirsty Cheyenne warriors. The masked man turned to his faithful Indian companion and said, "We're in trouble, Tonto."

Tonto replied, "You mean you're in trouble, *white man*."

Every time the U.S. Cavalry major rode through the Pawnee village, he'd wave to the aged Chief. In response, the old man would give him the finger, in the usual vertical manner. Then he'd turn his hand so that the same digit stuck out horizontally.

After a few weeks the major could stand it no longer. He rode over to the Chief and said, "Look, I know what it means to get the finger straight up, but what does it mean when you turn it sideways?"

"I don't like your horse, either!" grunted the Chief.

A tough old-time Indian fighter came staggering back into camp with seven Shoshoni arrows piercing his chest and legs. A doctor examined him and remarked:

"Amazing stamina. Don't they hurt?"

The old-timer grunted, "Only when I laugh."

An Arizona sheriff, seeking re-election, was out poli-tickin' around a Hopi Reservation when he came upon a group of women.

"Now, if you squaws will vote for me," he said, "I'll guarantee you full benefit of Social Security."

"What Social Security?" asked one woman.

"Well," said the sheriff, "that's a plan whereby you'll get about eighty bucks a month when you're sixty years old."

"Ugh?" muttered the squaw. "When sixty years old, one buck a month be enough for me!"

"Why do they call that Indian girl *Revere Ware*?"

"She's well-built, nicely rounded, and has a copper bottom."

Did you hear about the pioneer in the Dakotas in the 1870's whose horse came to a sudden stop?

Injun trouble.

A papoose strapped to his mother's back leaned out of his shelter and called to another papoose being carried in similar fashion, "How's your old woman on hills?"

Many, many moons ago the great Apache Chief Cochise was nearly ready to enter the happy hunting grounds. He called for Geronimo and Fallen Rocks, the two strongest and most courageous braves in the tribe.

"Each of you must go and seek buffalo skins," said Cochise. "One who get most skins will be the new Chief."

Within a month, Geronimo came back with 200 pelts but Fallen Rocks did not return. They searched for him diligently, but he was never found. However, Indians never give up hope. Even now as you drive through the Old West, you will see signs saying: WATCH FOR FALLEN ROCKS.

An Arapaho squaw was explaining the facts of life to her daughter. "Stork not bring papoose," she pointed out. "It come by beau and error."

Sitting Pretty: Sitting Bull's gay brother-in-law

A spinster schoolteacher on her summer vacation was visiting the reservation at Yosemite. She spotted a big brave standing against a tree and became very curious about his sex life.

"How does a great big man like you get satisfaction up here where there are no young squaws?" she asked.

The Indian stared at her unbelievingly and then said, "You see cow?"

"Yes, you don't mean . . . ?"

"Yes," said the brave, "me make love to cow. Look, you see horse?"

"Yes," answered the spinster, horrified.

"Me make love to horse."

"Oh, dear," cried the distraught old maid.

"No," grunted the Indian. "No make love to deer. Run too fast."

Several years ago when a poll was taken 15 percent of the Indians thought that the United States was right in getting out of Vietnam. Eighty-five percent thought they should also get out of America.

A Chippewa Chief once thought he had a perfect memory, and decided to make a deal with the devil. An agreement was reached whereby the Indian could have anything on earth he wanted if he could prove his case. If not, the devil would claim his soul. The devil asked one question, "Do you like eggs?"

The Chippewa answered, "Yes."

Forty years later there was a big pow wow of all the chiefs. The devil appeared in tribal costume, approached the Chief, raised his right palm in greeting and said, "How."

"Fried," answered the Indian.

No one blames the Indians for being discouraged. They were the only ones ever to be conquered by the United States and not come out ahead.

Chief Bald Eagle had married three wives and gave a wigwam to each of them. He promised that he would provide them with any kind of bed covering they wanted. The first was a practical girl so she asked for the hide of a buffalo, which was easily obtained.

The second, who was intelligent but daring, asked for the pelt of a bear. This was a little harder and more dangerous for him but the skin was nevertheless soon secured.

The third wife, who was the prettiest and most vivacious, asked for the skin of a hippopotamus. This was a real challenge to the Chief, but he finally succeeded in getting her one.

Nine months later the first wife had a boy, the second had a girl, and the third had twins, a boy *and* a girl. Which confirms that the squaw on the hippopotamus is equal to the squaws on the other two hides.

Comanche Catchphrase: Indian scalp enemies—
　　　　　　　　　　　　White man skin friends

Iroquoian Lad: Father, why I not named Tom or Jim
or Fred like white man?

Father: Indian boy named after last thing seen
before moment of conception: Running
Water, Standing Bear, like that. Why
you ask, Broken Rubber?

Meanwhile, back on the reservation, an Indian maiden
did a naked rain dance and made the Creeks rise.

Running Pony was arrested for murdering his wife. He
explained: "Me plant corn, come up corn. Me plant
potato, come up potato. Me plant Indian, come up
Chinaman. Me kill 'em squaw."

Indian Uprising: When Sitting Bull sat on a tack

The tourist stopped off at an Indian reservation.
Deciding to make friends with the Red Man, he hailed a
passing brave and said: "White man glad to see red
man. White man hope big Chief feel fine this morning."

The Indian stared, then yelled: "Hey, Harry, come
over here! This guy is terrific!"

In Arizona a movie producer hired a Hopi Chief to
predict the weather, thus saving money by not schedul-
ing any shooting on those days the Indian predicted
inclement weather. The cost was high, but worth it.

And for two weeks it worked. When the chief said
it was going to rain, it rained. When he said it would be
clear, it was clear. But then one day the Red Man didn't
submit his prediction. The producer visited the Indian.

"You've done great for us, predicting the weather
perfectly. Why is it today you can't tell us the
weather?"

"Radio broke," explained the Chief.

Marlene, a pretty Philadelphia secretary, was taking her first trip across the United States. Driving through the desert she ran out of gas. An Indian gave her a ride, sitting behind him on his pony. Every few minutes as they rode he let out a wild whooping yell that echoed across the desert. Finally, he deposited her at a gas station and went off with a last "Yah-hoo!"

"What were you doing," asked the station owner, "to make that redskin do all that hollerin'?"

"Nothing," said the girl. "I just sat behind him with my arms around his sides holding on to his saddle horn."

"Miss," said the man, "Indians ride bareback!"

ARAB

ARMAD, an unkempt rug peddler, made his way down a Cairo street trying to sell his wares. "Will you buy a carpet?" he pleaded to a passing tourist.

"No! No!" snapped the tourist, drawing back. "They stink."

"How dare you say that!" cried the Arab indignantly. "I'll have you know that my carpets do not stink! It's me!"

Ad agencies report that in the Arab countries the best-selling mouthwash has a roast lamb flavor.

Arab potentates use a hand-held device which puts the prod in position to satisfy a harem. Surely you've heard of the Sheik Injector Raiser.

Since time immemorial Arabian men have ridden majestically on their donkeys, while members of their harem, laden down with all sorts of burdens, trudged patiently behind on foot. After World War II, however, all that was changed. Harem wives were emancipated. They still carry the burdens, but now they walk in front. Explained the Arab, "There remain many unexploded land mines. . . ."

Women's liberation has become an integral part of Egyptian society despite the traditional disapproval of girls who date many different men. One night, Sabra was sitting in a car with a boy who began kissing her passionately while removing her dress. She started to sob.

"Why are you crying?" he asked.

"I'm afraid you will take me for the wrong kind of girl. I'm not that kind."

"Stop crying, I believe you!"

"You are the first man," sobbed Sabra.

"You mean I'm the first man to do this with you?"

"No. You are the first man to believe me."

Sheik: An Arab who crawls across the desert sands and makes five tracks

What happens to Egyptian girls who forget to take the Pill?

They become Mummies.

Oil has made Arabs even richer than the Texas "black gold" barons. One Arab just bought a car so big he had a putting green installed in the back seat.

Arab

The sexual urge of a camel
Is stronger than anyone thinks.
He's lived for years on the desert
And tried to seduce the Sphinx.

But the Sphinx's center of pleasure
Lies buried deep in the Nile
Which accounts for the hump on the camel
And the Sphinx's inscrutable smile!

Said the Arab to the anthropologist: "A young boy for a good time, a woman for sons, but for a good wife give me a camel every time."

The three Bedouin tribesmen had almost reached the oasis on their fleet camels when a hillock of sand suddenly loomed up in front of them.

Ali swerved around it to the left and Hassan did so to the right, but dauntless Abdul rode right up and over the obstacle—and straight toward a pair of hobbled camels engaged in lovemaking. The copulating beasts became frightened and broke apart at their climax. Just as Abdul swept by, the male of the pair showered him with the potential makings of millions of little camels.

"Poor Abdul," muttered Hassan, as their bespattered comrade came up to join them. "He doesn't know enough to rein in out of the come."

Queer Arab: One who speaks with tongue in sheik

Sheik Abdulla was looking for a few girls for his teenage son's harem. He asked a neighboring sheik, "Do you have any extra brides you'd like to sell?"

"Yes," said the neighbor, "I've got a few lying around loose."

The son nudged his old man. "Try to get some tight ones," he whispered. "Yours are all loose—loose as camels."

Unbeknownst to Sheik Amir, the magic bottle that he bought in the bazaar had once contained Mogen David wine; so the genie who appeared when the sheik rubbed it was, of course, Jewish.

"What is your wish?" asked the genie.

"I'd like my penis to extend to within a foot of the ground!" demanded the hot-blooded son of the desert.

So, quick as a wink, the Jewish genie shortened the sheik's legs.

Sheik Moustapha needed one more horse before setting off on a trip into the desert. Two steeds were brought to him from a nearby village, but the owner of each horse, not wanting to give up his animal, insisted his nag was worthless, broken-winded, old, and crippled.

"It's a simple thing to settle," said the sheik. "We will stage a race. The winning horse will be taken."

An advisor stepped forward and whispered: "It won't work, Your Highness. Neither man will let his horse ride fast."

"They will," said Moustapha. "Let each man ride the other's horse."

A whimsical Arab from Aden
His masculine member well laden,
   Cried, "Nuptial joy
   When shared with a boy,
Is better than melon or maiden."

Foster, lagging behind his tour group in a Cairo market-place, noticed a man on the ground brushing his camel.

"Excuse me," said Foster. "Do you know the time?"

The Arab reached over and held the camel's testicles. Then, moving them slightly, he said "Five before four."

Foster ran after his tour group and insisted, "You've got to come and see."

The group went back with him. Foster asked for the time. Again the Arab camel driver reached for the camel's balls. He seemed to be weighing them as he moved them to and fro. Finally, he announced, "Five minutes past four."

The others went on their way but Foster, still amazed, leaned over and said, "Listen, I'll give you twenty American dollars if you show me how you tell the time."

The Arab pocketed the money, and beckoned for Foster to kneel down where he was. Then he took the camel's balls and gently moved them to the side, out of the way.

"Do you see that clock over there?" asked the Arab.

BLACK

A white man parked on a street in Harlem found that the rear end of his car had been smashed in. On the windshield he found a note that said:

"Hey, baby, I just smashed your car. The folks that saw the accident are watching me. They think I'm writing down my name and address so you can contact me regarding the damage. They are wrong."

Black people love baseball. It's the only way a black man can shake a stick at Whitey and, what's more, get paid for doing it.

Have you heard about the new black "Welfare Doll?"
You wind it up and it doesn't work.

Leonora went into a drugstore to buy film. When she came out she was ripping mad.

"Rodney, you go into that store and cut that man real good," she said to her boyfriend.

"Why, honey," asked Rodney, "what happened?"

"I told him I wanted some film," she explained, "and he got the nerve to ask me what was the size of my brownie."

Did you hear about the redneck down south that broke the color line? He installed a black phone. Of course, he'd never call his sister on it.

Misery: When a Soul Brother catches his wife involved in Honkey Pankey

What is the difference between a white owl and a black owl?

At night when you walk through the forest, the white owl goes, "Who? Who?"

But the black owl says, "Who dere? Who dere?"

Mr. and Mrs. Jeeter were visiting a deceased relative's grave. They stopped in front of a tombstone and Mr. Jeeter carefully spelled out the inscription: "Not dead but sleeping." He chuckled and remarked to his wife, "Dat colored boy ain't foolin' nobody but hisself."

Alvin: What would you call a soul brother who became a millionaire cravat maker?

Curtis: A tie-coon.

The congregation sat in awed silence as the preacher thundered: "God didn't make no hell down below! He'd already made Georgia, so why waste any more time and space?"

A company had a policy against hiring blacks. Whenever a black applied for a job the personnel manager told him the firm was overstaffed. One day when he gave this excuse to a black applicant the fellow said, "That's all right. The little bit of work I would do wouldn't be noticed."

The treasurer of a black civil rights organization picked up the phone and heard a southern voice drawling on the other end of the line, "Hey there, boy, I want to talk to the head nigger."

Shocked and outraged, the treasurer said, "My dear sir. . . ."

"I want to contribute $50,000 to your cause, so let me talk to the head nigger," the redneck said.

"Hold the line there, brother," the treasurer said. "I think I see that ugly jigaboo coming in the door right now."

Lois: If yo' was rich, what would yo' want most of all?
Roop: An alarm clock wid a busted buzzer.

One day two Negroes bought a watch between them. It went wrong and one of them took it to pieces and found a dead fly inside.

"No wonder de watch wouldn't go," he said, "De engine-driver am dead."

Sick of American bigotry and of his nagging mother-in-law, Ashford went to New Guinea and became a cannibal. Six months later his mother-in-law tracked him down with a non-support summons. There was only one thing to do; he ate her.

Guess what? She still disagreed with him.

Did you hear about the Black Panther-gay lib group?
They are known as the African Violets.

Every time Wash Jones goes to a fancy restaurant he asks for a finger bowl so he can wash his spoon before he steals it.

Gardner and Williams, two students at a Southern university, met at the campus book shop. "Hey," said Gardner, "did you hear they just appointed a black man head of the department of Thermonuclear Reaction and Research Studies?"

"Yeah," said Williams, "someone already told me about the nigger."

An all-Negro team was playing an integrated team. During the excitement of the game, a player on the all-Negro team fouled a black member of the integrated team.

Angry at what happened, a white boy from the integrated team rushed up to the referee and yelled, "Did you see what that nigger did to our colored boy?"

A black man who had just died arrived at the Pearly Gates and was directed by Saint Peter toward a side entrance marked COLORED. "What's the matter with y'all up here?" the black man demanded to know. "Don't you know that down on earth times have changed? In Alabama where I'm from all the schools, neighborhoods, and churches have been integrated. Speaking of churches, just a few minutes ago I was on my way to be married to a white woman. Come to think of it, that's the last thing I remember."

"How you like the new preacher?"

"Don't like him much. He preached so long I couldn't keep awake and he hollered so loud I couldn't go to sleep."

35

Southern Preacher: Lis'en here, you awl, if'n we is
goin' to get money to build our
church we is gotta work harder.
Yo gotta work like beavers to get
sumthin' done.

Sister Rose: But pawson, beavers work with
their tails.

Preacher: Well, all reet!

The venerable Negro preacher had used the letters
B.S., M.S., and Ph.D. after his name for years without
ever having excited any comment from anyone in his
congregation. Finally one particular nosey biddie
questioned him about it.

"Well, sister," he answered, "you knows what B.S.
stand foh, don't you?"

"Of course, ah does," was the rather indignant
reply.

"Well den, dat M.S. jest means 'more of same' and
Ph.D. means 'piled higher and deeper.'"

A preacher was listening to a young man confess his
sins. In the middle of it he stopped him. "Wait a
minute, young man," he said, "you ain't confessin' —
you's braggin."

Buxom Luberta went to a rummage sale. She looked
around and swooped down upon a pair of red satin
slippers six AAA. Holding the pair up she asked, "How
much is these lovely red slippahs?"

"For you?" inquired the saleswoman.

"Yes, ma'am."

"Why they are much too small for you, and,
besides, one of them needs to have the heel repaired."

"That doan' matter," responded the black lady.
"Jes' think how fine they will look sticking out under
the aidge of mah bed!"

"I understand you've got your divorce, Jenny. Did you get any alimony from your husband?"

"No, Miz Moskowitz, but he done give me a first-class reference."

Black woman who is furious with her husband shouts at him, "You get your ass across the street!"

"Where do you think I've been getting it!" he replied.

Hall of Famer Satchel Paige, considered to be the greatest black pitcher of all time, talked as colorfully and spiritedly as he pitched. Here are some of his classic delicacies of wit:

"Avoid fried meats, which anger up the blood."

"If your stomach disputes you, lie down and pacify it with cool thoughts."

"Keep your juices flowing by jangling around gently as you move."

"Go very light on the vices, such as carrying-on in society; the social ramble ain't restful."

"Avoid running at all times."

"Don't ever look back. Something might be gaining on you."

And, of course, there is Paige's classic comment on Cool Papa Bell, dubbed the Ty Cobb of black baseball, who is also in the Hall of Fame:

"He was so fast he could turn out the light and jump into bed before the room got dark."

How do you circumcise a Negro?

With a jig-saw.

"Now, Sam, do you solemnly swear to tell the truth, the whole truth and nothing but the truth?"

"Ah does."

"Well Sam, what have you got to say for yourself?"

"Well, Jedge, wif all dem limitations you jes put on me, ah don't believe ah has anything at all to say."

The attorney was briefing his witness before calling him to testify. "You must swear to tell the truth, do you understand?"

"Yes suh, I'm to swear to tell the truth."

"Do you know what will happen if you don't tell the truth?"

"Ah expects our side'll win the case."

An old colored man was brought to court because he was behind in his alimony payments.

The Judge said, "Josh, you told me you'd pay Liza three dollars a week when I gave you the divorce and now you are only paying her a dollar-fifty. What's the trouble?"

Josh said, "Jedge, when I quit Liza to marry Mary I thought Mary was a better worker, but she ain't making as much money as I thought she would."

Judge: Mose, is your wife dependent on you?
Mose: She sho is, Judge. If I didn't go out and get de washin' she'd starve plum to death.

"Leroy," said the Judge, "do you think it's right to leave your wife hard at work over the washtub while you pass your time fishing?"

"Yas, suh," replied the black, "it's all right. Mah wife don' need any watchin'. She'll work jes' as hard as if I was dah."

"Mrs. Charles, you sure have three fine little daughters," said Mrs. Giovanni, her neighbor. "What are their names?"

"De first is Emerald, de second is Pearl, and de baby is Onyx."

"Why did you ever name the child Onyx?"

"Cause she was onyxpected!"

Moses: Does this lodge yo' belong to have any death
       benefits?
  Levi: Yessuh! 'Deed it does. When yo' dies, yo' don'
       hab to pay no more dues.

"Suh, can I have the evening off to go to lodge? It's
important, for I's de Sublime King."

"Why, you only joined the lodge two weeks ago,
and you tell me you're the Sublime King already?"

"Yessuh. You see, in our lodge, de Sublime King
am de lowest office dere is."

Employer: Ossie, did you go to your lodge meeting
         last night?
  Ossie: Nossuh. We dun have to pass on it.
Employer: How is that?
  Ossie: De Grand All-Powerful Invincible Most
        Supreme Unconquerable Potentate dun got
        beat up by his wife.

Jackson was jumping up and down on a manhole cover
on a street in Detroit, shouting: "Thirty-nine! Thirty-
nine! Thirty-nine!"

Along came Kowalski. "What you do?" he asked.

"Here man," said the black, "you jump for awhile."

Kowalski began leaping up and down on the
manhole cover. Suddenly, the black snatched the cover
away and the Polack fell into the sewer.

Jackson replaced it and, jumping up and down,
shouted: "Forty! Forty! Forty!"

PFC Perkins refused to go and fight in Korea. He was
told that if he would not bear arms the Provost
Marshall would shoot him.

"Are you a conscientious objector?" asked the first
Sergeant.

"I ain't objectin' to nothin'," said Perkins, "but I
had the gonorrhea and the diarrhea both, and if this
Korea is anything like it—go ahead and shoot!"

Did you hear that Alex Haley wanted to commit suicide?

He found out he was adopted.

Mrs. Vandermeer learned that her husband made overtures to the black housekeeper and that he planned to go to her bed that night. Mrs. Vandermeer substituted for the housekeeper whom she sent across town on a late errand unexpectedly.

Later, she is boffed like never before. Finally satisfied physically, and now wanting her revenge, she snapped on the bedside lamp.

"I'll bet you're surprised!" she said triumphantly.

"Ah sure is, ma'am," said the black chauffeur in her arms.

Through the years, Eddie Anderson, as Rochester, provided some of the biggest and best laughs on "The Jack Benny Show." The following is an exchange that Mr. Benny often quoted as being his favorite:

Rochester was raving about his new girl friend, telling how beautiful she was:

Jack: Well, Rochester, I've never heard you rave that much about any girl. Tell me, how beautiful is she?

Rochester: Do you want me to describe her to you?

Jack: Yes.

Rochester: Mr. Benny—did you ever see a Hershey bar with all the almonds in the right places?

The great Bill Robinson, the foremost black star of his time, used to get howls with this one: "A little colored soldier tried to break out of camp and was stopped by the guard. Our hero challenged the guard with, 'I've got a mother in Heaven, a father in Hell, and a girl in Harlem and I'm gonna see *one* of them tonight!"

Why are there so few blacks in Alaska?

They find it hard to grow watermelon up there.

Jelly Jive visited a house of prostitution. After he took his clothes off, the whore watched in amazement as he put a clothespin on his nose, cotton in his ears, and a prophylactic on his penis.

"Hey," she asked, "how come you putting a clothespin on your nose and cotton in your ears?"

"There's only two things I can't stand," replied Jelly Jive, "a gal screaming and the smell of burning rubber."

Alma was being interviewed by the welfare officer concerning her application for relief.

"Are you married?"

"Yes, suh, ah been married twice."

"Any children?"

"Sho' has. Ah got six."

"All by the same father?"

"Nawsuh! Ah had two by mah first husband, two by mah second husband, and two without any help from nobody."

Elmo drove Lena way out in the backwoods, parked his car, and said, "Awright now, honey! Is you gonna be a Chesterfield and satisfy or are you gonna be a Camel and walk a mile?"

"Brother," said Lena, "it all depends on whether you is regular or king size!"

One black girl asked another, "Do you know the zip code of your belly button?"

"No."

"Then how do you expect to get mail in your box?"

41

Willie D. left Harlem to visit friends in Mobile. On his second night there he met Laura Mae, a beautiful lady whom he soon led out in the woods. As they prepared to make love, Willie removed his pants and hung them neatly on a tree.

"You must be from the North," said Laura Mae.

"Right on, baby," said Willie, "but how could you tell?"

"A southern boy don't hang up his clothes, 'cause when we're finished we're gonna be three miles from here."

Afroletic Supporter: A soul brother's jockstrap

John Henry was about to indulge in his favorite pastime with Patrice, his Saturday night special.

She was lying in the sack having just given her chassis a job. "Say," said John Henry, "if you think I'm goin' down that slippery road without chains you're crazy!"

Sallie was suing a neighbor for slander. "What did the slander consist of?" asked the Judge.

"That woman told people I wasn't rich," she replied.

"I don't see how that can be a reflection upon your character," declared the Judge. "Even though a lady isn't rich she can still have a good reputation."

"That may be so," answered Sallie, "but that woman said I was pushed for cash."

"Ah say, Dinah, would you jes' s' soon—?"

"Looky ere, Jack Roberts, don' you git fresh wif me. Mah name's Miss Brown, not Dinah. Ah don't 'low only mah bes' and mos' intimate friends to call me Dinah."

"Ah begs yo' pahdon, Miss Brown. But say, Miss Brown, would you mind moving yo' ass a little to de lef'. One ob mah balls is cotched."

"Why, Mariposa, I haven't seen you in ages. I heard you got married. Is it so?"

"Is it so? I can't even touch it with a powder puff!"

African Roulette: You get in bed with six beautiful black girls and one of them is a cannibal

Back in the bad old slave-breeding days, a southern slaver borrowed Big Charlie, a famous black stud, from a friend who owned another plantation several hundred miles up the Mississippi from New Orleans.

Big Charlie impregnated fifty black wenches and returned home.

"How did it go?" asked his master.

"Fine, Boss," said the black stud, "but Ah cain't unnerstan' why ah had to bother wid all that travelin' jes fo' two hours' wuk."

It was a very hot day. Champ Chambers spied a shady tree, lay down under it and soon was fast asleep. A black snake crept up one of his trouser legs and fell asleep too. When Champ awoke he found a queer-looking head sticking out of his pants. He began pulling it out and the more he drew, the greater grew his amazement.

"I always knew you was black and I knew you was long," he said. "But where did you get those baby blue eyes?"

Black Family: A group of people with the keys to the same abandoned building

"Whom did the ancients believe supported the world on his shoulders?" the teacher asked.

"Atlas," one little girl answered.

"Correct." The teacher continued. "Now if Atlas supported the world on his shoulders, who supported Atlas?"

A little black girl shouted out, "Maybe his wife took in washing."

"How come you applying for a driver's license—you can't drive!"

"I know, man, but it comes in real handy for cashing bad checks!"

Harlemite Huckley was driving his big blue Cadillac through Mississippi. He pulled up at a gas station and honked his horn.

"What you want, boy?" asked the attendant.

"Give me ten gallons of gas," said Huckley. "Check my oil and wipe off the windshield. And look, man, I'm in a hurry."

Immediately the attendant pulled out a big .38, picked up an empty oil can and said, "You must be one of them smart ones from up North. I'm gonna show you boy, how we expect your kind to behave around here."

He threw the oil can into the air and emptied his gun at it. When the can came down, it had five bullet holes in it. The attendant tossed it to Huckley saying, "Now, you look that over and think about it."

Huckley looked at it, then got out of the Caddy and picked up an apple he had lying on the seat. He threw the apple up in the air, whipped out a knife and as the apple came down, he made a few passes at it. The apple landed at the attendant's feet, peeled, cored, and quartered.

The attendant said, "How many gallons of gas did you want, Sir?"

Thurmon, Pickens, and Diggs were discussing the world's greatest inventions. "I believe," said Thurmon, "that electricity is the best invention. It turns on the lights, makes the TV work, it do everything."

"Yeah," agreed Pickens, "but ah believe that atomic power is the most important invention. It can do everything electricity can and you can push a button and blow up the world."

"Well, gennamen," said Diggs, "to me the greatest invention is the Thermos. It keep da hot food hot and da cold food cold."

"What so great about that?" asked Thurmon.

"How do it know?" replied Diggs.

Alvin: What would you call a Negro maternity dress manufacturer?

Curtis: A mother frocker.

At a stag party in Harlem, Pearline was giving a "circus." She lay stripped on a matting and went through all the eye-rolling, bosom-heaving contortions of a woman with a lusty man screwing her. She wriggled her buttocks, locked and unlocked her thighs, squirmed and tremored.

Overcome with emotion one of the stags shouted: "Fuck her hot!"

Pauline stopped and turned toward the offender: "If you-all cain't be gentlemen," she said, "this performance cain't go on!"

Eager to change his luck, a white man approached Big Bessie.

"Ah charges ten dollars," said the hooker.

But the white man refused at that price, and also at five dollars.

"Well, then," said Bessie, "Yo' can have it fo' three dollars, but at that price Ah'm losin' money."

While rambling along the railroad tracks, Isaac found twenty dollars. He walked on a little further and felt his corns pinch. "Feet," he said, "I'm gonna buy you a brand new pair of shoes."

He continued his walk, but soon felt the hot sun on his forehead. "Old top," promised Isaac "I'm gettin' you a cool, shady hat."

Just then Isaac's stomach grumbled. "Okay, belly," he said, "I will buy you a fine meal."

Isaac resumed his journey. Five minutes later, he stopped in shock. He looked downward at the front of his pants and hollered: "Hey big stiff, who told **you** we came into money?"

Jet Set: What a soul brother carries in his jockstrap

The school teacher was complaining rather bitterly to Cornelia about the behavior of little Nathaniel.

"He's always picking on boys smaller than he is and beating them up," she said.

"My goodness," said Cornelia, "that boy is jest like his pappy."

"And several times I've caught him in the cloak-room with one of the little girls," continued the teacher.

"Jest the sort of thing his pappy would do!" conceded Cornelia.

"Not only that, but he steals things from the other children."

"The very same as his pappy. Lord, ah sure am glad ah didn't marry that man!"

Mistress: Were you entertaining a man in the kitchen last night?

Maid: Well, ma'am. I was doin' my best.

Two little colored boys met on the street.
"I'm five years old. How old are you?"
"I dunno."
"Do you ever think of women?"
"Naw!"
"Then you is four!"

Morris Schwartz was the only Jewish man living in a
small Texas town. He was loved by everyone. Schwartz
had given freely of his wealth and was particularly kind
to the black population. And then he died.

Since he had no relatives, Schwartz bequeathed all
his worldly goods to the townspeople. In order to show
their respect and appreciation they decided to bury
Schwartz in grand style.

They dressed him up in a cowboy outfit, complete
with ten-gallon hat and gold spurs. They had a solid
gold Cadillac built, placed Schwartz behind the wheel,
and then dug a hole large enough to accommodate the
car and its deceased occupant.

As they were lowering the Caddy into the ground,
two blacks stood nearby and one commented to the
other, "Ah tell ya, man, them Jewish folks sure knows
how to live!"

What do you get when an Irishman marries a Negro?
A guy they keep throwing out of the parade every
St. Patrick's Day.

When John married Theresa, they moved into an old
flat in Harlem. The first pieces of furniture the husband
brought home were a big wash tub, a washboard and a
full-length mirror.

"What's all that junk?" asked the wife.

"That's no junk—you take your choice. You take
the tub, and the washboard and go to work, or you take
the mirror and sit down and watch yourself starve!"

47

Cannonball Jenkins came home and found his wife,
Jermaine, naked and lying exhausted on a rumpled bed
with a towel thrown over the foot.

"What's goin' on, honey?" he asked suspiciously.

"I just had the misery something terrible," she
explained. "Couldn't get outa bed all day."

"An' what's dat towel doin' there?"

"I wrang it out in water to put on my head, dat's
all."

Cannonball slowly pulled out a large razor and
began stropping it.

"Whach you gonna do with dat razor?" asked
Jermaine nervously.

"Effen dat towel dries out soft," said Jenkins, "I'm
gonna shave!"

"How you makin' out with that good-lookin' blonde
Jewish model?"

"Real good!" replied Raymond. "Tonight I'm
plannin' to play Road Builder with her."

"What the heck is Road Builder?"

"I talk her into laying down and then I black top
her!"

"What do they call a guy who uses a pitch fork to
shovel cement?"

"A mortar forker."

Hannah had been seeing Cazzy on and off for many
years. Time passed and she had a child out of their
union. One day Hannah met Cazzy by chance and told
him she had named the baby Asphalt.

"Why'd you name him that?" he asked.

"Because," said Hannah, "it was my ass an' your
fault!"

Comedian Irwin C. Watson takes a gentle, self-mocking, cerebral approach to Blackness:

"I wasn't too surprised to hear there was a group starting a Back-to-Africa movement. They say that within the next ten years all the people of African descent will be goin' back to Africa. It warmed my heart. Every time I see one of them I wish him a pleasant voyage. See, 'cause I'm not goin'. I figure with all them goin' to Africa and all the white men goin' to the moon, they'll soon just be me, some Puerto Ricans and Chinese fightin' to keep those Indians on the reservation."

White man: I don't know what to do, my house has burned to the ground, my wife died, my car's been stolen, and the doctor says I gotta have a serious operation.

Black man: What you kickin' about, you white ain't you?

Buck (Washington) and (John) *Bubbles* (Sublett) were a great comedy team in the early Thirties. Here is a sample of some material that broke up audiences all over America:

Buck: Boy, I sure can run.

Bubbles: You sure can run all right. What was you runnin' up the street for this mornin'?

Buck: Oh, I was just runnin' to stop a fight!

Bubbles: Yeah, well who was fightin'?

Buck: Me and another fella!

Bubbles: Whatch' you wanna *run* fer?

Buck: You cra-a-zy? You don't think my legs is gonna stand around and see my body *abused*, do ya?

Bubbles: Yea, but why didn't you stay there?

Buck: Now there you go again. My father told me any time that I see somebody was gonna hit me—for me to leave there!

SIGN IN HARLEM HABERDASHERY
THINK YIDDISH
DRESS BRITISH

An NAACP official telephoned the Library of Congress and told the chief librarian that the library had 18,000 books with the word "nigger" in them and that all the books had to be removed in a week.

"But," protested the librarian, "we have fifty thousand volumes with the word 'bastard' in them."

"I know," said the official, "but you bastards aren't organized."

Naomi hit the numbers real big and decided to buy a mink with her winnings. As she stood in front of the store mirror, the mink down to her ankles, she turned to the white saleslady and asked, "Don't you think this coat makes me look too Jewish?"

Three boys, a Catholic, a Jew and a black kid, were sitting on a curb. A priest and a rabbi saw the boys.

The Catholic priest recognized one of the kids as a member of his parish. So, he said "Sonny, what are the two biggest things in your life?"

He said, "Father, the two biggest things in my life are the Catholic church and my priest."

The rabbi looked down and he recognized the Jewish kid from his congregation. He said "Son, what are the two biggest things in your life?"

"Rabbi, the two biggest things in my life are my congregation and my rabbi."

Both members of the clergy left smugly satisfied. Then the little colored kid looked at his two buddies and said, "Say, ain't neither one of you little mama's boys ever had no watermelon or girls yet?"

Black Tennis Player (to three white players): "Anybody for a game of mixed doubles?"

Two small boys, one Indian, the other a Negro, got into an argument over whose race had made the greatest contribution to America.

"We got Ralph Bunche and Jackie Robinson and Mohammad Ali," said the black boy. "You Indians ain't got anybody like that to show."

"Well, we had Jim Thorpe and Geronimo," said the Indian.

"But that was a long time ago!" snapped the black. "What have you people done for modern culture?"

"Awright," said the Indian. "How many kids are there in America?"

"Oh, about eleventy billion, I suppose."

"How many of them you ever seen playing Cowboys and Blacks?"

Did you hear about the black boys running toward their swimming hole, shouting, "The last one in is a dirty Polack!?"

The day after a black family moved into the neighborhood, their son Richie approached Sammy, a Jewish boy, who lived nearby. "We's as good as you are," announced the young black.

"Why is that?" asked the Jewish boy.

"You got a duplex house—we got one, too!"

A week later, Richie stopped Sammy again. "We's as good as you!"

"Is that right?"

"Yeah man! You got a Chevy Impala—we got one, too!"

Another week went by, and this time Richie said to his new friend. "We's better than you!"

"Why?" asked the Jewish boy.

"We ain't got no colored people living next door to us!"

51

Football is one of the most popular sports among black people. It's the only sport in the world in which a black man can chase a white man and 80,000 people stand up and cheer.

Lydell walked into a Chinatown tavern and said to the Oriental behind the bar, "Hey, Chink, give me a drink!"

Ten minutes later, Lydell called out again, "All right, Chink, give me a drink!"

A short time passed and once again Lydell shouted, "Say, Chink, give me a drink!"

"Listen," said the Chinese bartender, "I have held my temper. But you come behind the bar and see how you like to be insulted!"

The two men exchanged places. "Okay," said the Oriental. "Now, you nigger, give me a jigger!"

"Sorry," said the black, "we don't serve Chinks in here!"

CHINESE

HARRISON had just laid a wreath of flowers on a comrade's grave, and while crossing another section of the cemetery he saw a Chinese man lay some rice on the grave of a countryman.

"When do you expect your friend," asked Harrison, "to come and eat the rice?"

"When your friend comes to smell the flowers."

What do you call a Shanghai maid who inherits ten million yen?

A Chinese fortunate cookie.

Did you hear about the Chinese owner of an opium den who was so impressed by American business methods, he installed a credit plan?

And over the front door he put a big sign: FLY NOW, PAY LATER.

Reliable sources state that acupuncture fees in China are so modest they are referred to as pin money.

Glass: Chinese marijuana

At a U.N. banquet, Williams sat next to Kim Wah Low, the eminent Chinese diplomat.

Williams, trying to be nice, leaned over and made conversation.

"You likee soup?" he asked the Oriental.

Mister Low nodded his head.

"You likee stew?"

He nodded again.

Kim Wah Low was then introduced as the guest speaker and got up and delivered a forty-minute address on the UN definition of encouragement to self-reliance by underdeveloped countries of the world. The speech was in flawless Oxford English.

He returned to his place beside Williams, sat down, and said, "You likee speechee?"

Confucius say: Wife who put husband in dog house, soon find him in cat house.

Mr. and Mrs. Wong rushed to the hospital where Mrs. Wong was delivered of a 9-pound totally white baby.

Mr. Wong stood outside the nursery window, shaking his head sadly. "It must have been the milkman," he concluded, "two Wongs don't make a white."

Puzzled Chinaman: "Me can't understand why our child so velly white."

Wife: "Well, Occidents will happen."

"Name?" queried the immigration official.

"Sneeze," replied the Chinese proudly.

The official looked at him. "Is that your Chinese name?" he asked.

"No, Amelican name."

"Then, let's have your native name."

"Ah Choo."

Chinese Voyeur: Peking Tom

One of Hollywood's newer starlets hired a Chinese boy as servant and gave him instructions about what to do around the house. "Always knock at my door before you come in," she would say, "I may be dressing." A little while later the boy opened the door of her room.

"Didn't I tell you to knock first?" the starlet said. "How did you know I wasn't dressing?"

"Very simple," said the boy. "Before I knock, I look through keyhole."

A tough movie actress phoned the laundry: "Now I don't want any more of your nonsense. Get that laundry up here, and licketysplit."

"Bling laundly O.K., lady, but no licketysplit."

Chinese Casanova: Don Wong

A woman ran into the precinct station and screamed, "I was sexually molested by a Chinese laundryman."

"Wait a minute," said the desk sergeant.

"How do you know he was a Chinese laundry-man?"

"He did the whole thing by hand," she replied.

Did you hear about the ruptured Chinaman?

He was called Won Hung Lo.

"I went to a Chinese abortionist," the receptionist confided to a friend. "Everything worked out fine, but thirty minutes later I was pregnant again."

Said a Pekinese husband named Goon Yang,
"I top off each lunch with a noon bang.
   Desserts such as that
   Cannot make a man fat,
And besides—what is sweeter than poontang?"

Kung Fu Yung: It's just like Egg Foo Yung, except that you have to wrestle the waiter for your order

The big trouble with a Chinese bomb is that one hour after you explode one, you want to explode another.

The message in the fortune cookie read, "You will meet a cute redhead. You will give her money. She is our cashier."

Red Chinese Colonel: General, I agree this attack plan will work, but it will cost us 350,000 men.
General: So, what's the problem?

Foong, the laundryman had been in America ten years and kept sending money to his wife in China, telling the bank clerk proudly that his wife has just had a new baby.

"But, Mr. Foong," said the clerk, "You've been here in America ten years."

"Yes, yes," says the Chinaman happily. "I got velly good fliends in China."

Said the Chinese girl when she was issued the marriage license: "It won't be wrong now!"

Potter saw a store with a sign reading, HANS SCHMIDT'S CHINESE LAUNDRY.

Being curious, he entered and was greeted by a Chinese who identified himself as Hans Schmidt.

"How come you have a name like that?" asked Potter.

"When I land in Amelica I stand in immigration line behind German," explained the Oriental. "When they ask German his name he say, 'Hans Schmidt.'

"When official ask me my name, I say, 'Sam Ting.'"

A newsman sent a letter home from Red China. At the end he put a note, "I hope this letter reaches you. The censors are very tough."

When the letter arrived, another note had been added, "There are no censors in the People's Republic of China."

In China when the subscriber rings up the exchange, the operator may ask: "What number does the honorable son of the moon and stars desire?"

"Hohi, two-three."

Silence. Then the exchange resumes:

"Will the honorable person graciously forgive the inadequacy of the insignificant service and permit this humbled slave of the wire to inform him that the never-to-be-sufficiently censured line is busy?"

Did you hear about the two Burmese girls looking for a Mandalay?

Landers and his girl friend were dining at the famous House of Hunglo. Landers said to the waiter, "Bling us some flied lice."

The waiter left and returned with won ton soup. They ate it, and Landers again said to the waiter, "We want flied lice."

This time the waiter brought them two orders of egg roll. As the waiter walked away, Landers called loud enough for everyone in the restaurant to hear, · "How about that flied lice?"

The Chinese waiter came back to the table and said, "Can't you pronounce fried rice—you plick?"

There were three Chinese girls that never married. They were No Yen Tu, No Wan Tu, and Tu Yung Tu.

Caldwell finished his five-course Cantonese dinner in Kowling's Restaurant and then opened the fortune cookie. It said: "Better tip big—we've got the bomb, too."

Walters walked into a Chinese restaurant and saw a Negro waiter. Surprised, he asked what was the specialty of the house.

"Pizza!" said the Black waiter.

"Pizza!" cried the customer. "In a *Chinese* restaurant?"

"Can't help it!" said the waiter. "This is a Jewish neighborhood."

MESSAGE INSIDE A FORTUNE COOKIE
PLEASE DISREGARD PREVIOUS COOKIE

Trusting Red China is difficult for one very simple reason: Any country that has more than 750 million people and maintains that ping-pong is its favorite sport will lie about other things, too.

Oriental Grocery Clerk: A chinese checker

A telephone operator in San Francisco says that the city's Chinatown receives fewer calls than any other area of similar size in the city. And with a straight face, she explained the reason:
    "I guess there are so many people named Wing and Wong that people are afraid they'll wing the wong number."

Chiang Kai Chek was being interviewed on Formosa by a reporter for UPI. "When was the last time you had an election, General?" the journalist asked.
    "Just before bleakfast," winked Chiang.

A western miner, desperate for a prostitute, was told by the bartender that there was no woman in the mining town, but that he could use "the Chinese laundryman."
    "Will anyone know?" he asked.
    "Of course not," reassured the bartender, "only the five of us."
    "Five of us? Why five?" questioned the miner.
    "Well, you'll know. And I'll know. And the Chinaman will know."
    "Yes, but that's only three. Who're the other two?"
    "Oh, they hold the Chinaman."

Did you hear about the two Chinese faggots?
    They had a tong war.

Then there was the Chinese prostitute who soon found herself the richest whore in town—her customers kept coming back two hours later!

Chinese Proverb: Teach your son in the hall and your
wife on a pillow

Lu Ting ate at a Greek restaurant because Papadopoulos, the owner, made really good fried rice. Each
evening he'd come in he would order "flied lice."

This always caused Papadopoulos to fall down
with laughter. Sometimes he'd have two or three
friends stand nearby just to hear Lu Ting order his
"flied lice."

Eventually the Chinese's pride was so hurt that he
took a special diction lesson just to be able to say
"fried rice" correctly.

The next time he went to the restaurant, he said
very plainly, "Fried rice, please."

Unable to believe his ears, Papadopoulis asked,
"What did you say?"

Lu Ting shouted, "You heard what I said, you
fluckin' Gleek!"

DUTCH

W HAT do they all Ex-Lax in Holland?
Dutch Cleanser.

Did you hear about the Dutch boy who stuck his finger
in a dyke?
She punched him right in the mouth.

Bill Dana's whimsical creation, Jose Jimenez, always
reproduced with affection the Hispanic speech
patterns:

Interviewer: Jose, what do you do for a living?
Jose: I am the Dutch representative.
Interviewer: Oh, something to do with tulip bulbs,
windmills?
Jose: No, just something to do with Dutch—
you know, Plymouth, Chrysler, Dutch.

ENGLISH

A woman in an English court, charged with shoplifting, was asked by the magistrate if she had anything to say on her own behalf.

"Yes, sir, I have," she replied hopefully, "I take only British goods."

Seaman Clanford was asked by a French sailor why the British Navy always was victorious.

"That's easy to answer," replied the Briton. "We always pray before we start fighting."

"But so do we," retorted the Frenchman.

"Yes," said the sailor, "but we pray in English."

The visitor to London was thoroughly disgusted. "Rain, rain, rain, fog, fog, fog," he shouted at his guide. "When do you have summer in England?"

"I say," replied the guide, "that *is* a difficult question. Last year it came on a Wednesday."

Mrs. Appleby, a thoroughly English lady, took her just-married daughter aside. "Always remember, dear," she cautioned, "that the marital act is the most unspeakable, reprehensible thing in the world."

"But mother," said the bride, "you had six children."

"Yes, dear, I simply closed my eyes and thought of England."

Connoisseurs of coition aver
That the best British girls never stir.
   This condition in Persia
   Is known as inertia;
It depends what response you prefer.

An elderly gentleman with a walrus mustache, frock coat, and bowler hat jiggled the telephone receiver. "I say, operator," he said, "I want to talk to Sir Reginald Barrett, in Grosvenor Square, London."

"I'm afraid I can't hear you, sir," said the operator.

"Sir Reginald Barrett, Grosvenor Square, London," said the party.

"I still can't hear you," said the operator. "I guess you're English, aren't you?"

"My dear madam," said the gentleman, "if I were any more English I couldn't talk at all."

"You English are just too reserved," said the American.

"Nonsense," said the Englishman. "Why I rowed for Cambridge some years ago and I knew all the other fellows very well—all except one, that is, and of course, he was away up in the bow."

"I know why the sun never sets on the British Empire. God wouldn't trust an Englishman in the dark."

                          —Duncan Spaeth

Armbruster, an American importer, went to London to discuss the import of some tea from England. In spite of a really good offer, the staid old English firm seemed to take a dim view of the deal. Armbruster couldn't figure them out and finally he cornered Farnsworth, an ancient official.

"Say," asked Armbruster, "what's standing in the way of this deal, anyhow?"

"Well, of course this must remain strictly confidential, sir," said Farnsworth, "but we've had a bit of trouble over there in the past."

"Really?"

"Why, yes," said the old Englishman. "They dumped one of our shipments of tea into Boston Harbor."

"With all due reverence, my boy, I really think our English custom at the telephone is better than saying 'Hello' as you do in the United States."

"What do you say in England?"

"We say, 'Are you there?' Then, of course, if you are not there, there is no use in going on with the conversation."

When the nude Lady Godiva returned from her famous ride through Coventry she was met by her husband.

"Where have you been?" he asked.

"You know perfectly well," answered Godiva, "I have been riding quite naked through the streets in order to shame you into reducing those dreadful taxes of yours."

"I know, but that damned horse of yours got back two hours ago."

Extensive research has revealed that the expression, "Hooray for our side" was first heard from the crowds lining the streets when Lady Godiva made her famous ride sidesaddle through the streets of Coventry.

Harry, who grew up in Philadelphia, was making his first visit to England. One night he spotted a ravishing young redhead in a pub, walked over to her and stated conversationally, "You know, I come from the other side. . . ."

"Let's go right to my flat," she exclaimed, "This I gotta see!"

An American walked up to a Briton at a bus station and asked him,

"Could you tell me where Piccadilly Circus is?"

The Englishman replied, "Yes, I could," and calmly got onto the bus.

A Londoner and a Californian were on a ship returning to America, and the American was criticizing the British way of life.

"The trouble with you English," he ranted, "is that you stick together too much. There should be more intermingling. In my blood there's Russian, Spanish, Greek, and Italian."

"I say," said the Britisher, "that was very sporting of your mother."

A visitor to New York from England was finding America much more different from the "mother country" than he'd suspected.

"You Americans!" the Briton commented dryly. "You order hot tea, then put ice in it to make it cold, then you put sugar in it to make it sweet, then you put lemon in it to make it sour, then you lift your glass, say 'here's to you,' then you drink it yourself!"

Englishman: Odd names your towns have. Hoboken, Weehawken, Oshkosh, Poughkeepsie.

American: I suppose they do sound queer to English ears. Do you live in London all of the time?

Englishman: No, indeed. I spend part of my time at Chipping Norton, and divide the rest between Bigglewade and Leighton Buzzard.

A London chap sees a good-looking girl sitting alone at another table and says, "Would you care for a cigarette?"

She said, "Sorry, I don't smoke!"

He waited for a few moments and then said "Would you care for a drink?"

"Sorry, I don't drink!"

He waited another ten minutes and asked, "Would you care to have dinner with me?"

"I'm sorry," she replied, "I don't eat dinner!"

"Well, for heaven's sake, if you don't smoke, or drink, or eat dinner, what in heaven's name do you do about sex?"

"Oh, along about six I have a cup of tea and a biscuit!"

Teacher: What are the races that have dominated England since the invasion of the Romans?

Small Boy: The Grand National and the Derby.

During the heavy bombardment of Portsmouth in the early days of the blitz, an air-raid warden ran up to the opening of a public shelter and shouted, "Are there any expectant mothers down there?"

"Hard to say, sir," replied a feminine voice. "We've only been down here a few minutes."

Sir Reginald, riding in a New York taxi, was challenged by the driver to solve a riddle: "This person I'm thinking of has the same father that I have and the same mother, but it is not my sister and it's not my brother. Who is it?"

The Britisher thought for a moment and then gave up. "It's me," the cab driver told him.

"By Jove, that's jolly good! I must try that on the chaps at my club!"

A month later, he was sitting in London with his cigar-smoking cronies. He said, "Gentlemen, this individual I have in mind is not my brother, and not my sister, yet this person has the same parents as I have. Who is it?

After several thoughtful minutes, all the members conceded defeat. "Who is it?" one of them inquired, "Come, Reggie, give us the answer."

Reggie slapped his knee in triumph. "It's a taxicab driver in New York City!" he roared.

Baxter, a British newspaperman, got back to London after touring the U.S. for his paper. His fellow correspondents clustered around him one day wanting to learn something about recreation and amusement of Americans. "Well," said Baxter, "Americans play a lot of strange games, but there's one called Damn-it."

"No, it couldn't be," exclaimed the newspaperman.

"Yes, it's true. It's played in auditoriums. Hundreds of people fill the seats and have small numbered cards on their laps. A man on stage calls out a lot of numbers, and finally one person jumps up and shouts, 'Bingo!' And all the others exclaim, 'Damn-it!'"

"Sir Charles," asked Lord Witherspoon, "did you hear that joke about the Egyptian guide who showed some tourists two skulls of Cleopatra—one as a girl and one as a woman?"

"No, let's hear it," replied Witherspoon.

67

King Arthur left his queen well strapped into a chastity belt when he went off to war. The belt had an opening large enough for any penis, but inside was a guillotine blade, acted upon by a spring when the penis entered.

When King Arthur returned, he examined all the Knights of the Round Table, and not one of them had a penis except the gallant Sir Galahad. Tearfully grateful, the king offered Sir Galahad any reward he cared to ask, for his fidelity.

"Half my kingdom, if you want," said King Arthur, "name it and it's yours!"

But all Sir Galahad could say was "Ug, glop, glop!"

> To his wife said Sir Henry de Dawes,
> "Fix this chastity belt round your drawers!"
>   But an amorous Celt
>   Found the key to the belt
> While the Squire was away at the wars.

Two camels slowly approached each other in the desert, their riders identically dressed in excessively long Bermuda shorts and tropic helmets.

They pause, and the riders speak: "English?"

"Of cawss."

"Foreign service?"

"Cinema photawgraphy."

"Oxford?"

"Cambridge."

"Homosexh'l?"

"Certainly nawt!"

"Pit-y!"

And the two camels continued their separate ways across the desert.

Sir Reginald Farthington was on trial before the high court of Australia for the crime of molesting an ostrich.

"Before passing sentence," announced the Judge, "Do you have anything to say?"

"Your honor," said the Englishman, "if I'd have known you were going to make such a fuss about it, I'd have married the bloody bird!"

Two English gentlemen of the old school were discussing old acquaintances one evening in their London club.

"What," asked one, "ever became of old Cholmondeley?"

"Why didn't you hear? Cholmondeley went to Africa on a game hunt, and by Jove, the chap took up with an ape!"

"An ape? Is the old boy queer?"

"Heavens, no! It was a female!"

It is little known that Sherlock Holmes had a secret vice unrevealed in the stories. When Dr. Watson came around to 221B Baker Street one afternoon, the housekeeper told him that Holmes had a visitor, a schoolgirl.

Watson sat down to wait, but then heard muffled sounds coming from the study. Fearing that the schoolgirl might be an assassin in disguise, he broke open the door, only to find the great detective and the girl—a very young girl—engaged in rather a shocking form of play.

"By God, Holmes," huffed the doctor, "just what sort of schoolgirl is this?"

Smirked Holmes, "Elementary, my dear Watson."

When the Queen had her baby, she was being offered congratulations by hundreds of people, when a certain gentleman walked by. "You're a fine-looking man," said Her Majesty, "What do you do for a living?"

"I'm a photographer," he replied.

"Isn't that remarkable," said the Queen. "My brother-in-law's a photographer."

"Isn't that remarkable," he said, "My brother-in-law's a queen."

The American soldier stood on a London street corner.

A pretty blond from Soho passed by, and a gust of wind lifted her dress higher than was decent.

"A bit airy," remarked the friendly soldier.

" 'Ell yes!" retorted the Cockney girl. "What did you expect—feathers?"

Sir Henry, bored with the English country life, visited a French *salon de plaisir*. In response to Sir Henry's request for something unusual, the Madame suggested, "I can give you Hott Tung, a Chinese delicacy."

"No," replied his lordship, "I've already had one of those."

"Perhaps," asked the Madame, "you'd like to make a selection from our Black African group."

"I've had one of those, too," yawned Sir Henry. "Actually the only thrill I haven't tried would be a little bitty girl, about eight years old."

"This is outrageous!" shrieked the Madame, "The very idea is criminal! I'm going to summon a police-man."

"No, don't do that," said the Englishman, "I've already had one of those!"

An old ship's carpenter was giving a lecture on technical details to army officers preparing the invasion of France during World War II. He was continually interrupted when he pronounced words like "helm" and "hash" as the names of trees, by a very la-di-dah voice from one of the officers correcting him. "You mean elm, of course, and ash, don't you?"

Finally, exasperated, the old carpenter said, "Now, 'ere we 'ave the hoak."

"You mean oak, of course!"

"O'coss. It is the very finest wood to use for pounding piles into piers. And for the benefit of our young friend 'ere, I don't mean pushin' 'emmeroids hup the harses or hanuses of the Haristocracy!"

"What a big family you have, Mrs. Flaume," said the visitor to Brighton.

"Yes'm. And the funny thing is that all the names begin with a haitch. "Ther's 'Orace, 'Erbert, 'Enry, 'Ugh, 'Ubert, 'Arold, 'Arriet, and 'Etty—all except the last one, and we 'ad 'er named Halice."

The Queen was traveling in England's back country when she saw a man, his wife, and a flock of children. Impressed, the Queen asked, "Are all of these your children?"

"Yes, your Highness," answered the man.

"How many children do you have?" asked the English sovereign.

"Sixteen," was the reply.

"Sixteen children," repeated Her Highness. "We should give you a knighthood."

"He has one," piped up the lady, "but he won't wear it."

Welsh Rarebit: A Cardiff virgin.

Alfie and Dan, two Cockney pub crawlers, were in their cups one afternoon when Alfie pointed to a woman sitting at the end of the bar.

"Hey!" he said, "That woman looks like Queen Elizabeth!"

"Nah," replied Dan. "What would the Queen be doing in a pub in hogtown?"

"I'm telling you it's her," insisted Alfie. "Can't you see the resemblance?"

"Look, that ain't the Queen," said Dan. "And I'm willing to bet five on it."

"You're on," came the reply. "I'll go ask her." He walked over to the woman sitting at the bar and said, "I beg your pardon, are you the Queen?"

"Get lost, you little runt," growled the woman, "before I kick your ass across the room!"

He returned to his seat. "Well?" his friend asked.

"Well, she didn't say she was and she didn't say she wasn't."

Once upon a time an English girl retired at the age of thirty with five million pounds—all because she knew how to handle her dukes.

Colonel Effingham was walking to his club late one night when a beautiful black hooker stepped out of the shadows, linked her arm in his, and said, "How would you like to take me home?"

"Good heavens, girl," exclaimed the Colonel, "all the way to Africa?"

Sir Cedric and Lord Griffin, the big African game hunters, were having lunch.

"I say old man," harumphed Sir Cedric, "I do believe the word is spelled 'w-o-o-m-b.'"

"No, Ceddie, old bean," answered Lord Griffin, "I'm really quite sure it's spelled 'w-o-o-o-m-b.'"

"Begging your pardon, sirs," said the waitress, who had overheard the conversation, "but I believe the word is spelled 'w-o-m-b.'"

"Well, old chap," said Sir Cedric to his companion, "it is quite plain that this young lady has never heard a large elephant relieve itself!"

Did you hear about the lady lawyer from London who dropped her briefs and became a solicitor?

Bertie and Reggie, two young students from Oxford, out for a night on the town, picked up a couple of gals in a dimly lit pub and began touring the town. In one spot, while the girls were occupied in the ladies' room, one of the men whispered to his companion, "I say, old man, would you mind awfully if we switched dates?"

"Not much," said the other. "But yours seems a decent sort of girl; what's wrong with her?"

"Nothing much," replied the first, "but between the smog and the grog and the fog, I seem to have picked up an aunt of mine."

During World War I, RAF Captain Bainsby shot down the German ace Baron Von Ribsten over English territory. The next day Bainsby visited the Baron in the hospital.

"Old chap," said the Britisher, "is there anything I can do for you?"

"Yes," replied Von Ribsten, "they are amputating my right arm. Would you drop it over Germany?"

Captain Bainsby did as he was requested and a week later returned for a visit. "My friend," said the Baron, "they are taking off my right leg. Would you drop it over the Fatherland?"

Bainsby fulfilled the request and went back to see his air nemesis once again.

"Captain," said Von Ribsten, "they are going to remove my left leg. Once more, can I get you to drop it behind the German lines?"

"Of course, old bean," replied Bainsby, "But, I say, you're not trying to escape are you?"

Minimum: A tiny British mother

Winston Churchill sat in a first-class train compartment. Across from him an elderly Englishman with monocle and school tie was reading the London *Times*. For half an hour neither man spoke. Then the old gentleman lowered his paper and bleated, "Name Churchill?"

"Yes," replied the famous statesman.

"Winston?"

Churchill nodded.

A long silence followed as the white-haired Englishman stared over his paper at Churchill. Finally he broke the silence.

"Harrow '88?"

"Yes," said Winston.

"Ah," said the old gentleman. "Now I place you.

An elderly Englishman was sitting quietly in his London club when an old friend came up and said, "Sorry, old boy, to hear that you buried your wife yesterday."

"Had to," replied the other man. "Dead, you know."

This English sportsman had been abroad and returned to his home without notice. While walking through the corridor with his butler, he looked into his bedroom and discovered his wife making love to a strange man.

"Fetch my rifle at once," he instructed his butler.

In a matter of minutes his rifle was brought to him and he raised it to his shoulder taking aim, when he was tapped by the butler who whispered, "If I may say so, sir, remember you are a true sportsman. Get him on the rise."

The Duke woke up in a very manly condition. He summoned Jeeves.

"Ah," said Jeeves, when he saw what he hadn't seen in months. "Shall I summon the Duchess?"

"Oh, no!" said the Duke. "Just fetch me a pair of very baggy trousers. I'm going to try to smuggle this thing into London."

Three slightly deaf Englishmen were motoring to London in an old, noisy car. As they were nearing the city, one asked, "Is this Wembly?"

"No," replied the second, "this is Thursday."

"So am I," put in the third. "Let's stop and have one."

English

An Englishman, a Frenchman, and a German were arguing about the respective merits of their languages.

The Frenchman said, "French is the language of love, the language of romance, the most beautiful and pure language in the world."

The German announced, "German is the most vigorous language, the language of philosophers, the language of Goethe, the language most adaptable to the modern world of science and technology."

When the Englishman's turn came, he said:

"I don't understand what you fellows are talking about. Take this (and he held up a table knife). You in France call it *un couteau*. You Germans call it *ein Messer*. We in England simply call it a knife, which, all said and done, is precisely what it is."

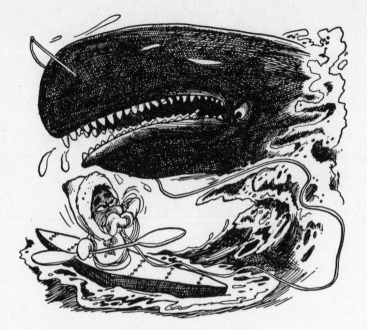

ESKIMO

A tourist in Nome, Alaska seeing his first Eskimos, noticed a native mother with a blond, blue-eyed baby slung to her back and asked, "Is your child a full-blooded Eskimo?"

"Half," replied the native.

"Half Irish? Half Scotch? Half what?" asked the visitor.

"Half Coast Guard," said the mother.

Igloo: The stuff you use to stick to IGS together

Crawford was driving through the Yukon's northern-most navigable region. Suddenly, he stopped the car. An Eskimo was sitting in a sled tethered to two puppies, which the Eskimo had tied there to keep the infant dogs from running off.

"My God!" exclaimed Crawford. "Do you really expect those little puppies to pull that sled with you in it?"

"Sure," said the Eskimo smiling sardonically. "I've got a whip."

The super-duper salesman had accomplished a miracle. He had sold an icebox to an Eskimo. Several months later, he ran into the customer in town. "How's the refrigerator I sold you?" he asked.

"Fine," said the Eskimo. "But my wife hasn't got the knack yet of chopping up the ice squares to fit in them little trays."

The three explorers wandered over tundra after tundra until they finally came to an Eskimo village, where, nearly frozen to death, they were taken to the igloo of the leader. They huddled in a corner when the chief entered and handed them a small, thin blanket.

"What good's this little blanket gonna do us?" asked one of the men.

"You may need it," said the chief. "It gets a little cool at night."

"Boy, the weather's murder in Alaska."

"How cold does it get?"

"It's so cold in Alaska that the Eskimos go to Siberia for the winter."

What's the difference between a eunuch and an Eskimo?

A eunuch is a massive vassal with a passive tassel, while an Eskimo is a rigid midget with a frigid digit.

Harrison was one of the handful of men left behind to look after the Alaska pipeline. On his night off he wandered into the local house of ill repute which had just opened. The place was run and staffed by Eskimos. Harrison figured he was in for a great old time—but the girl he picked would only give him a nose job.

Father Duffy was sent to a small Eskimo village in the coldest part of Alaska. Several months later, the Bishop paid him a visit. "How do you like it up here among the Eskimos?"

"Just fine," replied the priest.

"And what about the weather?" asked the Bishop.

"Oh, as long as I have my rosary and my vodka I don't care how cold it is."

"I'm glad to hear it. Say, I could go for a bit of vodka myself right now."

"Absolutely," said Father Duffy. "Rosary! Would you bring us two vodkas?"

FRENCH

THE lady's French maid was leaving to get married. Madame said, "Juliette, I am overjoyed for you. You will have it much easier now that you're getting married."

"Yes, Madame," Juliette replied, "and more frequently as well."

Did you hear about the French groom who was so exhausted by the elaborate wedding reception that he fell asleep the minute his feet hit the pillow?

Mrs. Flabeau shouted at her husband, "Pierre! You have a mistress!"

"But no, *cherie*, I have no mistress."

"Don't lie to me, Pierre. This is the third time this week you washed your feet."

The following ad appeared in the personal column of a London paper:

"My husband and I have four sons. Has anyone any suggestions as to how we may have a daughter?"

Letters poured in from all over the world. An American wrote: "If at first you don't succeed, try, try again."

An Irishman sent a bottle of Scotch with instructions to drink the entire contents before retiring.

A German offered his collection of whips.

A Mexican recommended a diet of tacos and refried beans.

An Indian proposed yoga.

A Frenchman merely wrote: "May I be of service?"

An American and a French bride were discussing love.

"A Frenchman is very subtle when it comes to love," the French bride explained. "He begins by kissing the fingertips, then he kisses the shoulder, then back to the neck. . . ."

"Boy," the American bride interrupted, "by that time an American husband is back from his honeymoon."

Armand, whose fiancée had been seen kissing his friend Louis, sent Louis a letter asking him to appear for a duel so that he could avenge his honor.

Louis replied with a note saying, "Dear Armand, I have received a copy of your circular letter; and will be present at the gathering."

WORK SCHEDULE OF THE FRENCH CABINET

Monday:	Conference with leading personalities.
Tuesday:	Formation of new cabinet.
Wednesday:	First meeting of new cabinet.
Thursday:	First announcements of new cabinet.
Friday:	Withdrawal of announcements.
Saturday:	Resignation of new cabinet.
Sunday:	Holiday.
Monday:	See above.

A man took a cab to the palace of the Prime Minister, where he asked the driver to wait for him. The driver refused, saying he didn't have time.

"But you will wait for me," said the passenger, "I am the new Prime Minister."

"In that case," replied the driver, "I'll wait. You won't be in there long."

Pièce de Resistance: A French virgin

During a debate in the French Chamber of Deputies, one of the members was pleading for laws that would liberalize the legal standing of women.

"After all," cried out the speaker, "there is very little difference between men and women."

The entire Chamber of Deputies arose and shouted, *"Vive la difference!"*

They learn fast in France. When the little French girl was asked what the difference between *"Madame"* and *"Mademoiselle"* was, she replied without a moment's hesitation, *"Monsieur."*

A rural Frenchman was on trial for killing his wife when he found her with a neighbor. Upon being asked why he shot her instead of her lover, he replied,

"Ah, *m'sieur,* is it not better to shoot a woman once than a different man every week?"

Three young French boys from Paris were spending their summer on a farm in Normandy. One day, as they were walking by a hay field, they caught sight of the milk maid and the farm hand in the hay stack and stopped to watch.

"Ah," said the seven-year-old, "look at the grownups fighting."

"You are in error, my friend," replied the sophisticated eleven-year-old. "They're making love."

"Yes," agreed the thirteen-year-old, "and badly."

Why won't France ever have an astronaut?
Whoever heard of a Frenchman going up?

An American G.I., standing outside Notre Dame Cathedral in Paris, saw a magnificent wedding procession enter. "Who's the bridegroom?" he asked a Frenchman standing next to him.

"Je ne sais pas," was the reply. A few minutes later, the soldier inspected the interior of the cathedral himself, and saw a coffin being carried down the aisle. "Whose funeral?" he demanded of the attendant.

"Je ne sais pas," said the attendant.

"Holy mackerel," exclaimed the soldier. "He certainly didn't last long."

French kissing is like a toothpick. You can use it on either end.

From la France zair vunce ze young man
Zat got fresh on ze beach at ze Cannes.
  Zaid ze Mademoiselle,
  "Eh! Monsieur! Vot ze hell!
Stay away from vair eet ees not sun-tan!"

Toussaint, a French dignitary, was being shown New York City by the Mayor. As they arrived at the Empire State Building his honor said, "It's the tallest in the world! What do you think of it?"

Toussaint gazed at it admiringly and commented, "It reminds me of sex."

"That's a strange reaction," frowned the mayor. "How can the Empire State Building remind you of sex?"

The Frenchman said, "Everything does."

Mademoiselle Hookere, the Parisienne streetwalker, had an evening appointment with her psychoanalyst.

When she arrived at his office, the headshrinker asked, "Will you lie on the couch?"

Charlotte replied, "If you don't mind, I'd rather stand—I've been working all day."

Tyler, an oil baron from Texas went into a public *pissoir* in Paris. A Frenchman was standing at one of the urinals and began ogling the Texan's huge penis. Finally, Tyler turned to him angrily and began, "Say, bo. . . ."

The Frenchman looked down at his appendage. *"C'est beau? C'est magnifique!"*

A French chef was brought to America by a Texas millionaire at his wife's insistence.

One day the Texan found the chef performing cunnilingus on his wife.

"How do you like that!" he cried. "First he screws up my eating, and now he's eating up my screwing!"

Fellatio: The French connection

A stranger strolled into a New York bar and ordered a glass of cognac with a slice of limburger cheese. He finished the drink, but didn't touch the cheese. "Another, please," he told the bartender. Again he downed the cognac without eating the cheese.

When he called for a third, the barkeeper asked, "How come you're not nibbling your rat fodder?"

"I'm from France," explained the man. "When we drink over there, we have a lady of the evening beside us. That's why I wanted the limburger—to make me feel at home."

Clauseau and Vignon were arguing over the meaning of the phrase *savoir-faire.*

Cleaseau: "If you're screwing another man's wife and he bursts in and sees what's going on and says, 'Go ahead!' and you *can* go ahead—that's *savoir-faire.*"

How many men in the French Army?
About half.

In a girl's college French class, during a discussion of the last world war, the topic of *"Femmes de guerre"* came up.

"What is a *'femme de guerre?'*" asked one co-ed.

"It is a certain type of woman who, in times of war," replied the spinster teacher, "finds it quite profitable to station herself in a place easily accessible to the common soldier."

"Oh," said the girl. "I thought they were *'hors de combat.'*"

Frenchman: A man who kisses other fellows on
cheeks, and girls on all fours

The Madison Avenue exec was dallying with both his secretary and the French maid. On one particular evening he called home to make his excuses for a night out with the secretary.

Fifi, the French maid, answered the phone and the executive said in a very businesslike manner, "Tell Madam she'd better go to bed and I'll be along as soon as I can."

"Oui, Monseiur," purred Fifi, "and who shall I say is calling?"

SIGN ON OFFICE BULLETIN BOARD
OUR MISTLETOE WAS IMPORTED FROM FRANCE THIS YEAR,
SO THE CUSTOM OF KISSING WILL BE ALTERED TO SUIT

Linda: So in Paris I met this masseur . . .
Cindy: Not masseur, but Monsieur. A masseur is a guy
     who rubs you, pinches you, squeezes you, and
     massages you all over.
Linda: Like I said—I met this masseur. . . .

The subject was lovemaking. For weeks Arthur had
successfully answered all the questions asked him on
the television quiz show. He was now eligible for the
jackpot prize of $100,000. For this one question he
was allowed to call in an expert. Arthur chose a world
famous lover from France. The jackpot question was:
"If you had been king during the first fifty years of the
Assyrian Empire, which three parts of your bride's
anatomy would you have been expected to kiss on your
wedding night?"

The first two answers came quickly. Arthur
replied, "Her lips and her neck."

Now stumped for the answer to the third part of
the question Arthur turned frantically to his expert.
The Frenchman threw up his hands and groaned,
"*Alors, mon ami.* Do not ask me. I have been wrong
twice already."

Sitting at a cafe in Paris, Roger, an American, and
Pierre, a Frenchman, were arguing about how many
positions exist for intercourse.

"There are one hundred and one," insisted Roger.

"No," challenged the Frenchman, "there are one
hundred!" He then began reeling off an astounding list,
ending his hundred with doing it in the ear, while hanging from a chandelier.

Now it was the American's turn to enumerate.
"Our first way," he said, "is for the woman to lie on her
back and the man to lie on top of her—"

"*Oo la la!*" exclaimed Pierre, "ziss I nevir heard
of!"

The difference between American and French girls is just this: They both know what men like, but the French girl doesn't mind.

Watson, a Clevelander in Paris, was unable to find a bordello so he asked a gendarme to give him directions. The policeman did not understand English very well. Watson tried pidgin English and pointing.

"Me. . . ." he said pointing to his chest.

"Ah, you weesh to eat!" says the gendarme.

"No, no," said Watson. He tried again, taking out a twenty-dollar bill.

"Ah, you weesh to gam-bol?"

"No, no, no!" shouted the American in disgust, and he took out his penis.

"Ah, *oui, oui*," says the gendarme.

"Wee-wee, my ass! Where the hell is the nearest whorehouse?"

SIGN IN FRONT OF THE GEORGE V HOTEL IN PARIS
YANKEE GO HOME—BUT NOT UNTIL YOU'VE DONE ALL YOUR SHOPPING

A Parisian streetwalker was trying to seduce an American serviceman who couldn't speak French. When he finally took out his pecker she said, *"Oui! Oui!"*

"Wee-wee, nothing! It's the biggest one in our regiment."

One evening an American tourist in France was arrested for allegedly driving while under the influence, and then was given a breath test at the gendarmerie. "Well?" he asked, somewhat belligerently, as the old desk sergeant slowly read the findings and began to enter them on the arrest report.

"Disappointing, Monsieur," said the cop, shaking his head. "Chateau Duvalier . . . 1962 . . . rather thin . . . has not aged well."

Frenchman's Dream: To be reincarnated as a flea and
have his wife come back as a dog

What is the French art of self-defense called?
Tongue Fu.

Did you hear about the French girl who came to the
United States but soon returned home?
She missed her native tongue.

Claude was sitting at a sidewalk cafe sipping a glass of
wine. Just then his friend Rene came running up to him.
"Claude," he gasped, "I just saw a man going into
your house."
"Who is this man, Rene? What did he look like?"
"He was six feet tall and had black hair and a black
mustache," reported Rene.
"And did he wear a checked cap with a striped
Basque shirt?" asked Claude.
"*Oui,*" agreed Rene. "You have described the
man."
"That was only Pierre," he said. "He will make love
to *anybody!*"

Nicolle: I'll never forget the night my husband dis-
covered my great love.
Isabelle: What happened?
Nicolle: He beat the hell out of him.

The Perfect Lover: A Frenchman with a nine-inch
tongue who can breath through his
ears

Grant had gone to France on vacation, met a pretty French girl, married her, and returned home with his bride to Cleveland. After being in this country only three weeks the poor little Parisian went to a clinic for an operation.

On coming out from under the ether, she asked the doctor, "How soon can my husband and I resume our usual sex life."

"I'll have to look in my medical book," gulped the physician. "You're the first patient who's asked me that after a tonsillectomy."

Monsieur Foucard was visiting London for the first time. While walking about, he felt nature calling and looked around for a public latrine like those in Paris. He couldn't find one and, in desperation, stepped into a dark building entrance. Immediately, a Bobby tapped him from behind.

"You cahn't do that 'ere, you know."

Later he tried to go behind a tree but another Bobby stopped him. In a few minutes he was again prevented by a policeman.

Finally he noticed a shingle:
DR. DINGLEY, UROLOGIST.

Dashing into the office, Foucard said, "Doctor, I cannot—how you say—relieve myself!"

The doctor handed him a bottle and told him to step behind a screen. In a few seconds the Frenchman cried, "Doctor, another containair, *s'il vous plait!*"

The doctor handed him one and in a few minutes, had to repeat the process.

When the now happy Frenchman stepped out, the doctor asked, "My good man, who told you that you could not relieve yourself?"

"Ze entire London Police Department!"

GERMAN

"Finally the world has forgotten Germany's participation in World War II."

"How can you say that?"

"Today, German travelers can go anywhere in the world and be accepted. Of course, they tell everyone they're Swiss."

Did you hear about the new German microwave oven?
It seats twenty-five.

Helga and Inga were talking. "I'm going out with Kurt Wolfschmidt tonight," Helga confided.

"He's an animal!" warned Inga. "He'll tear your dress right off you!"

"Thanks for telling me," replied her friend. "I'll be sure to wear an old dress."

What is the German word for brassiere?
Stopenzefloppin.

In Leipzig, where one third of all street names have
been changed since the Russian occupation, trolley
conductors are required to call out both old and new
names to make it easier for visitors to find their way.

The other day the conductor of a car passing
through the center of the city made the required
announcement, "Karl Marx Square, formerly Augustus
Square."

A passenger, about to alight, shouted back, *"Auf
wiedersehen,* formerly Heil Hitler!"

German Pimp: A man who lives by the sweat of his
Frau

A German was fishing on the west side of a river in
Germany, and a Russian was fishing directly opposite
him on the east side of the river. The German was
catching plenty of fish, the Russian none.

"How come you catch so many fish?" asked the
Russian.

"Because," said the German on the western side,
"the fish over here are not afraid to open their mouths."

The film *The Longest Day* was a big hit in Germany.
The trick was, they ran it backwards so the Nazis came
out winning.

Danzinger was employed in a baby carriage factory and
his wife asked him to steal a buggy for their new infant.

He refused to do this but agreed to take sufficient
parts to make a complete machine.

The great day for assembly of the parts came and
after five hours, the wife went out to their backyard

and found her husband in a state of exhaustion.

"It's no good," said the German. "It always comes out a machine gun."

Cummerbund: A German sex club

During the days of Hitler's dominance, five Germans sat a a table in a coffee shop, each thinking his own thoughts. One of them sighed, another groaned aloud. The third shook his head desperately, and the fourth man choked down the tears.

The fifth man, in a frightened voice, whispered, "My friends, be careful! You know it is not safe to talk politics in public."

During the early Thirties in Germany a member of the Gestapo passing a restaurant saw this sign in the window:

BECAUSE OF HITLER
OUR PORTIONS ARE LITTLER

The SS man confronted the woman owner and made her take it down. The following week he was walking by the restaurant he found this sign:

BECAUSE OF HESS
OUR PORTIONS ARE LESS

Infuriated the agent forced the woman to remove it. Two weeks later the Nazi passed the eatery and was amazed to see yet another sign:

BECAUSE OF GÖRING
I'M GOING BACK TO MY OLD PROFESSION

A famous German comedian was sent to a concentration camp for being a little too truthful in his barbs.

At a nightclub in Munich, he said, "Ninety-eight percent of the Germans are for Hitler—but it's a funny thing, I keep running into only the other two percent."

Der Fuhrer didn't trust the reports he had been getting, that the people were still loyal to him. One evening he disguised himself and went to a movie house. Soon the newsreel went on. The announcer said: "And now the latest pictures of our great, our benevolent Dictator." The commentary went on. The picture flashed on the screen. With one motion, the audience rose in salute, shouting "Heil, Hitler!"

Hitler was so pleased with the response that he forgot to get up. The man behind him tapped him on the shoulder and whispered: "I know how you feel about the bastard, but you'd better stand up or the police will arrest you."

On one of his late-night shows, Dick Cavett cracked: "I just found a German-Chinese restaurant. The food is delicious. The only problem is an hour later you're hungry for power."

During the first years of World War II, when Hitler was getting ready to lead one of his armies into action, his valet told him, "Whenever Napoleon led his men into battle, he always wore a red suit. That way they could never tell if he had been wounded and was bleeding."

"Quick," the Fuehrer ordered, "go get my brown pants."

On the first day the Nazis occupied France a German soldier raped beautiful Josette. When it was over he said to her, "In nine months you will have a son. You may call him Adolph."

"In nine days you will have a rash," replied the Frenchwoman. "You may call it measles."

Hitler was having bad dreams, so he ordered his henchmen to find him someone to interpret them for him.

"Ah," intoned the seer, "I see that you are destined to die on a Jewish holiday."

Hitler frowned, but he was curious. "Which one?" he asked.

"It doesn't matter. Any day you die will be a Jewish holiday!"

The Nazi leader Göring was seated next to a fine blonde Aryan fraulein at a very important state dinner. During dessert he began feeling her leg under the table.

As his hand moved up her thigh he heard a hoarse masculine whisper, "Don't be surprised when you get to my balls—I'm Secret Agent X-Seven!"

GREEK

NEW YORKER Wilson was gazing into the crater of a Greek volcano. "It looks like hell," he commented.

"Oh, you Americans," said the guide, "you've been everywhere."

What happens when two Greeks get together?
    They open up a restaurant.

"Why were the Romans such great warriors?"
    "I dunno—why?"
    "Because they were afraid to retreat. They couldn't turn their backs on the Greeks."

How do they separate sailors in the Greek Navy?
    With a crowbar!

What do you call a Greek faggot?

Andros, Miklos, Vassilis, Giorgos, Manos, or just plain, "Hey, you!"

Did you hear about the Greek soldier who reenlisted in the army because he didn't want to leave his buddies behind?

The sign that's posted in each Greek bus
Sure fills the men with cheer.
They all obey it without a fuss
It says, "Step to the driver's rear!"

What's a Grecian urn?

About twenty-five dollars a week—unless he owns the restaurant.

The famous Greek ship owner, Ori Oristotle, was having a house built on a large piece of land in Greece. He said to the architect, "Don't disturb that tree over there because directly under that tree is where I had my first sex."

"How sentimental, Mr. Oristotle," said the architect. "Right under that tree."

"Yes," continued Ori Oristotle, "and don't touch that tree over there either. Because that's where her mother stood watching while I was having my first sex."

"Her mother just stood there while you were screwing her daughter?" asked the architect.

"Yes," said the Greek ship owner.

"But Mr. Oristotle, what did her mother say?"

"*Baaa*."

The Greek truck driver had just lugged a thirty-pound bunch of bananas up five flights of stairs.

"That'll be four bucks, lady," he told his customer.

Smiling, the woman let her robe slip all the way open. "Wouldn't you like some of this instead?" she asked slyly.

"Sorry, lady," he said, "but I'll have to ask my partner. Already this week, we screwed away four truckloads of bananas."

Greek: A man who enlarges the circle of his friends

Stanis, the luncheonette owner, was bragging to a friend. "If I had all of Onassis's money, I'd be richer than Onassis."

"How is that?" asked the friend.

"I'd still keep my luncheonette!" replied Stanis.

When the nearsighted Nancy first met Kazantzakis she thought he looked like a Greek God.

But now that she has been fitted with contact lenses she thinks he looks like a Goddamned Greek.

He's a Greek architect. Specializes in lunchrooms.

Kramanakis immigrated to New York. He got a job through relatives who taught him to say, "Apple pie and coffee," in English so he could order in a restaurant. The next day, Kramanakis walked into a diner. "What'll ya have?" asked the waitress.

"Applea pie anna coffee," said the immigrant.

Since that was all he could say he was forced to eat applie pie and coffee every day for a month. When he complained to his cousins, they taught him to say, "Ham sandwich."

Armed with the new addition to his vocabulary Kramanakis said to the waitress, "Ham sandwich."

"White or rye?" asked the girl.

"Applea pie anna coffee," said the Greek.

Did you hear about the Greek fishing trawler that had been out to sea for six weeks? None of the crew had seen each other face to face.

Andreas and Marcus were having a terrible fight. "You can go to hell this minute and if I never see your face again it'll be too soon!" shouted Andreas.

"You can take yourself and shove it up you-know-where!" screamed Marcus.

"Oho!" yelled the other Greek. "So now you want to make up!"

What's the difference between a Greek and a suppository?
There is none.

Zeno and Artemis were talking about books.
"My favorite novel is *Lolita,*" said Zeno. "It's the story of a love affair between a mature man and a twelve-year-old."

"Yes, go on," said Artemis eagerly, "a twelve-year-old what?"

Marika, a young Greek girl, was desperately unhappy in America. She walked down by the harbor one night and decided to throw herself into the sea. A sailor noticed her, heard the story and took pity on her.

"Look," he said, "I'll stow you away on my ship. I'll hide you in the life boat and every day I'll bring you food." Then he winked. "I'll take care of you, and you take care of me."

The girl understood his meaning immediately and she agreed. He sneaked her on board the boat, and hid her in a life boat. Every night he brought her food and they would make love. This went on for weeks. Then, one day, on an inspection tour, she was discovered by the captain. Weeping, she told her story of wanting to get home.

"And every night," she concluded, "this nice sailor come and I screw him and he screw me."

"He sure did, lady," said the captain, "this is the Staten Island Ferry."

GYPSY

Czechoslovakian, Bulgarian, Hungarian, Rumanian, Yugoslavian

How do you make a Hungarian omelette?
First, steal two eggs. . . .

How come gypsies are so good at seeing the future?
Their fathers have crystal balls.

You hear about the Gypsy family who won a million dollars in the sweepstakes?
They moved into a store on Central Park West.

What do they call an abortion in Prague?
A canceled Czech.

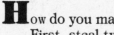

What do you say to a naked Bulgarian in the shower room?

Say nothing. Just get out of there as fast as you can.

And then there was the Hungarian lady who bragged around the local village that her son had become a liver specialist in America.

Pressed to tell the truth, she admitted that Mikhail was working for a butcher in New Haven.

Hungarians are notoriously lazy. When Laszlo got married he told his wife that marriage and a career don't mix well, so he hasn't worked a single day since.

The Gypsy girl told her father she wouldn't marry the man he chose for her unless he drove a long black Cadillac, would cover her in diamonds, and had a twelve-inch penis.

The father left in a rage. In a few hours, he was back. "Okay," he told her, "the car is parked outside, here are the diamonds, and the doctor cut off the three extra inches."

Why did the old Gypsy woman disown her son, the vampire?

Because he was getting to be a pain in the neck.

What is the difference between an umpire and a Gypsy?

An umpire watches steals and a Gypsy steals watches.

What happened when the Gypsy caravan was attacked by Indians?

First, they drove all the wagons into a circle, and then they sold them to the Indians.

When does a Gypsy make his violin cry?
When he returns it to the rightful owner.

Madison walked into Madam Sophia's Fortune Telling Parlor, took one look, and said, "Hey, you know your crystal ball's got three holes in it?"
"Certainly," she said, "I also give bowling lessons."

How does a Gypsy count his money?
In the dark.

Hilda was very worried because she had two green spots between her legs. She became so upset she finally went to a doctor who examined her thoroughly.
"Madam," said the physician, "it is obvious you are married to a Gypsy."
"That's right," replied the woman.
"Well," said the doctor, "you'd better tell your husband his earrings aren't made of gold!"

In Yugoslavia the Communists were conducting a purge. An old Gypsy was brought before the commissar. "How long," asked the commissar, "have you been in the Party?"
"Many years, Commissar."
"And your father?"
"Oh, he was a member, too, and my grandfather and my great-grandfather."
"Now listen," said the commissar dubiously, "back in those days there was no party."
"Oh, that didn't make any difference," replied the Gypsy, "we were stealing anyway."

Did you hear about the wealthy Gypsy who owned a chain of empty stores?

What is a Gypsy caravan?
A lead wagon and four stolen cars.

Madam Zobanga billed herself as both an expert ventriloquist and fortune teller. One day Mrs. Anderson, dressed in black, entered her parlor.

"Can you put me into touch with my dead husband, Walter?" asked the customer.

"You bet I can," promised Zobanga. Mrs. Anderson had such a soul-satisfying conversation with Walter that instead of paying the twenty dollar fee requested, she gave the Gypsy two twenties.

"This is very nice of you," said Madam Zobanga, "and just to show my appreciation, the next time you speak with your dead husband Walter, *I'm going to drink a glass of water at the same time.*"

What do you call a Gypsy who doesn't lie, cheat, or steal?
Deceased.

The Gypsy violinist gave his first music lesson—how to steal a violin.

It is a historical fact that Diogenes went all around the known world, lamp in hand, trying to find an honest man.
When he got to Hungary, they stole his lamp.

What did the Gypsy boy do with the hubcaps he stole?
He gave them to his mother to use for earrings.

Mrs. Kornfeld, aged seventy-two, was passing what used to be an empty store and noticed that it was now occupied by Madam Tanya, THE WORLD'S FOREMOST FORTUNE TELLER. Mrs. Kornfeld walked in and asked for help. The Gypsy promised she'd be able to contact the elderly woman's mother in the great beyond for fifty dollars.

Mrs. Kornfeld gladly paid the money. She and Madam Tanya then joined hands in the darkened room. As the Gypsy summoned the spirit, a vision suddenly appeared and greeted Mrs. Kornfeld.

"Mama," she gasped. "What is it like in your new life? Are you happy?"

"Yes, I'm happy," the vision answered. "Everything is very nice up there. But why have you sent for me to come back down here? Is there something you wanted to ask me?"

"Yes, Mama," said Mrs. Kornfeld. "But first tell me something else."

"What is it, my child?" asked the vision.

"Mama," said the Jewish woman, "where did you learn to speak English?"

IRISH

Gallagher and McCroy, never too fond of work, were strolling up a street in Donegal when they picked up a newspaper. The headline read: MAN WANTED FOR ARMED ROBBERY IN DUBLIN.

"Now if that job was only in Donegal," said Gallagher, "I'd take it!"

What's an Irish family's night on the town?
Bailing out dear old dad.

"Pat, what did you get for your birthday?"
"A pair of opera glasses."
"Are they any good?"
"Fine. See that church over there, about a mile away? Well, these glasses bring it so close that ye can hear the organ playing."

O'Houlihan got on a bus with a pipe in his mouth. "Hey," shouted the driver, "don't you see that sign up there, 'No Smoking Allowed?'"

"I'm no smokin' aloud!" said O'Houlihan.

"Smoking not permitted, wise guy," said the driver. "You're smoking! You got a pipe in your mouth!"

"I have my feet in my shoes," said O'Houlihan, "but that doesn't prove I'm walkin', does it?"

Muldoon and Nolan met in a Belfast pub. "I hear you got a letter from your brother, Denny, that went to America," said Muldoon.

"Faith, an' I did that," answered Nolan.

"An' what did the boy say about hisself?"

"I can't tell you," said Muldoon. "On the outside of the envelope was printed, 'Return in Five Days,' so I sent it back to him."

McGrath: I bought one of them new insurance policies.
Buckley: Is it any good?
McGrath: Great! You pay premiums for 40 years and if you're killed in a railroad accident, you get an income for life!

Bryant caught a tiny fish, which suddenly began to speak. "I'm really an elf and if you release me I'll grant you and your wife any three wishes."

So the Irishman released the fish, rushed home and told his wife. The couple was anxious to get to town and look at things to wish for, so the wife decided to make a quick dinner out of a can of beans. But she couldn't find the can opener and said, "I wish I had a can opener." *Kazam!* She had a can opener.

"You wasted one wish on that stupid can opener," screamed Bryant. "I wish it was up your ass."

And the sad part of the story is that they had to use the third and last wish to get it out again.

Doctor: Did that cure for deafness help your brother?
   Pat: Sure enough; he hadn't heard a sound for
         years and the day after he took that medicine,
         he heard from a friend in America.

"It's no use to feel my wrist," said Sean when the
doctor began feeling his pulse. "The pain is not there,
sir, it's in my head entirely."

Mrs. Kernan: I haven't been feeling meself lately!
Mrs. Malone: It's a good thing—that was a nasty habit
              you had!

"I'm gonna miss old Clance," said Muleen outside the
funeral parlor.
   "Yeah, he was a gentleman. He always took off his
hat before he beat up his wife."

Hennessy, loaded to the gills, was lurking on a dark
and deserted street corner. Soon a man came walking
by, and Hennessy sprang out of the shadows, a gun in
his hand.
   "Shtay where you are," he slobbered. Then he
pulled a bottle out of his pocket. "Here," Hennessy
ordered, "take a drink of thish."
   Too terrified to resist, the poor schnook took the
bottle and drank deeply. "Wow!" he exclaimed, "That
stuff tastes awful."
   "I know," gurgled the crocked Irishman. "Now you
hold the gun an' force me to drink some."

Irish Clubhouse: A brothel

What's the Irish version of the Chariots of the Gods?
   A hearse and a paddy wagon.

EPITAPH FROM EIRE
BENEATH THIS STONE LIES KILEY
THEY BURIED HIM TODAY;
HE LIVED THE LIFE OF RILEY
WHILE RILEY WAS AWAY.

"Mooney got rich quick, didn't he?"

"He got rich so quick that he can't swing a golf club without spitting on his hands."

Gannaway and O'Casey arranged to fight a duel with pistols. Gannaway was quite fat, and when he saw his lean adversary facing him he objected.

"*Debab!*" he said, "I'm twice as large as he is, so I ought to stand twice as far away from him as he is from me."

"Be aisy now," replied his second. "I'll soon put that right." And taking a piece of chalk from his pocket he drew two lines down the fat man's coat, leaving a space between them.

"Now," he said, turning to O'Casey, "fire away, and remember that any hits outside that chalk line don't count."

Why do Irish wakes last three days?

They want to make sure the Irishman is really dead —and not just dead drunk.

During World War II, Donovan refused to join the army. "It's not my war!" he contended. "It's England's war!"

That night as he was entering his favorite London pub, just as he put his hand on the door knob, a bomb dropped by the Luftwaffe destroyed the entire building.

Next day, he showed up at the army enlistment center.

"What changed your mind?" asked the sergeant.

"The bloody Germans," shouted Donovan, "blew a saloon right out of me hand!"

McBride and Kavanaugh were in a cafeteria sitting near the WATCH YOUR HAT AND OVERCOAT sign. McBride kept turning every minute, nearly choking on his food, to look at his overcoat.

Kavanaugh continued eating, paying no attention to his own coat on the hook. But McBride's constant twisting began to irritate him. "You dope," he said, "stop watching our overcoats!"

"I'm just watching *mine*," said McBride. "*Yours* has been gone for half an hour!"

The traveling salesman was boffing a local girl in a hayloft in a small Irish village.

Warming to his work, the salesman tried to kiss Colleen.

"No, don't do that," she begged. "Isn't what we're doing bad enough?"

"Sure, an' I ain't no party man, Dennis. I vote every time for the best man."

"An' how can ye be tellin' who's the best man, 'till the votes be counted?"

"Do you think if I poured you some gin again,"
Asked Finnegan, "You might care to sin again?"
   Said she with a grin,
   "If you want it back in
You must pay me a fin again—Finnegan!"

Here's one about the great Irish playwright, George Bernard Shaw:

A British woman who spent her life chasing celebrities once sent him a formal note that read: "Mrs. Wellington Mason-Fipps will be at home Tuesday between two and four o'clock."

The sharp-tongued Irishman sat down and scribbled off a note and sent it back. It said:

"So will George Bernard Shaw!"

"I see where your daughter Kathleen finally got married," said Mrs. Ryan.

"Yes," said Mrs. O'Callahan, "but I can't say as I much care for the man she married."

"What's the matter with him?" asked Mrs. Ryan.

"At the ceremony," explained Mrs. O'Callahan, "when the Father asked him did he take this girl in marriage, he answered in such a loud, nasty manner, that my poor sweet little daughter almost had a miscarriage!"

An Irishman is never at peace except when he is fighting.

"Was your father very shy, Rian?"

"Shy? My mother told me that if he hadn't been so shy I'd be five years older now."

Lanahan, an Irish political prisoner, escaped from jail by digging a tunnel that opened into a school playground. As he emerged in the open air Lanahan couldn't help shouting at a small girl. "I'm free—I'm free."

"That's nothing," she said, "I'm four."

IRISH TOMBSTONE
THIS MONUMENT IS ERECTED IN MEMORY OF
PATRICK CALLAHAN WHO WAS ACCIDENTALY STABBED
AS A TOKEN OF AFFECTION BY HIS LOVING WIFE

"Heat," explained Moynihan to his friend Mulligan, "makes things expand and cold makes them contract."

" 'Tis mad you are entirely," said Mulligan. "Whoever heard the like of that?"

"Well," replied Moynihan, "how do you account for the longer days in summer and the shorter ones in winter?"

Mrs. O'Donovan herded her large family into a cinema and explained to the cashier which of them was entitled to half-price.

"Those two," said Mrs. O'Donovan, "are under ten, those two are under eleven, those two are under twelve, those two are under thirteen and the older twins won't be fourteen until next week."

"In the name of St. Agnes, the virgin martyr," said the dazed cashier, "do you and your husband have twins every time?"

"Not at all," blushed Mrs. O'Donovan, "sure lots and lots of times we don't have any children at all."

Pregnancy: As in, "She's got the Irish toothache again"

An unshaven, bedraggled panhandler, with bloodshot eyes and teeth half-gone, asked Horgan for a dime. "Do you drink, smoke, or gamble?" asked the Irishman.

"Mister," said the bum, "I don't touch a drop, or smoke the filthy weed, or bother with evil gambling."

"Okay," said Horgan, "if you'll come home with me I'll give you a dollar."

As they entered the house, Mrs. Horgan took her husband aside and hissed, "How dare you bring that terrible-looking specimen into our home?"

"Darlin'," said Horgan, "I just wanted you to see what a man looks like who doesn't drink, smoke, or gamble."

The first gay bar was finally opened in Dublin. Every Gaelic in town goes there. It's called: SODOM AND BEGORRA.

Finnerty was marching in the St. Patrick's Day Parade for a half hour when he heard over the loud speaker, "You are now passing Rupert's Brewery!"

"Not me!" shouted Finnery and dashed out of line.

Cudahy, grogged to the gills, stood watching the St. Patrick's Day Parade. Unconsciously, he dropped his lit cigarette into an old mattress that was lying at the curb.

Just then the gray-haired members of the Women's Nursing Corps came strutting by. At the same time, the smoldering mattress began giving off a dreadful smell.

Cudahy sniffed a couple of times and declared to a nearby cop, "Officer, they're marchin' those nurses too fast!"

The great Fred Allen once described St. Patrick's day in New York as "the day when one million Irishmen get the chance to go north of Forty-Second Street."

St. Patrick's Day Cocktail: Two of them and you are Dublin over

Gaffney staggered into a bar crying. "What happened?" asked Brady the bartender.

"I did a horrible thing," sniffed the drunk. "Just a few hours ago I sold my wife to someone for a bottle of scotch."

"That is awful," said Brady. "Now she's gone and you want her back, right?"

"Right," said Gaffney, still crying.

"You're sorry you sold her because you realized too late that you love her, right?"

"Oh, no," said the Irishman, "I want her back because I'm thirsty again!"

Comedy writer Pat McCormick, one of the most brilliant Hollywood wits, ad-libbed this gem one night on the Johnny Carson Show:

"I was in a small town once that was so small the St. Patrick's Day Parade consisted of me, an Irish setter, and the guy in town who owned three Dennis Day albums."

What's the difference between a harp and a glass of beer?

An Irishman makes a harp tinkle and a glass of beer makes an Irishman tinkle.

"What were your husband's last words?" the funeral director asked Mrs. McCarthy.

" 'I don't see how they can make this stuff for five dollars and forty-nine cents a quart," she sobbed.

"Taggert was told by his doctor that he had better taper off on his alcohol consumption."

"What'd he do?"

"He switched from Four Roses to Three Feathers."

"Halt!" cried the sentry. "Who's there?"

"Friend with bottle of bourbon," was the reply.

"Pass, friend! Halt, bottle!" the sentry commanded.

Poteen is an Irish illegal brew that can burn holes in steel plate. After a pint of it Flaherty saw so many animals in his room that he put a sign on his house, FLAHERTY'S ZOO.

The local sergeant went to reason with him and was no sooner in than he was offered a glass of the Mountain Dew. When policeman staggered out thirty minutes later he raised his hand for silence.

"Ish all right men. The worst's over. He sold me half the elephants."

111

Bartender: Here, you haven't paid for that whiskey
you ordered.
Ramsey: What's that you say?
Bartender: I said you haven't paid for that whiskey
you ordered.
Ramsey: Did you pay for it?
Bartender: Of course I did.
Ramsey: Well, then, what's the good of both of us
paying for it?

The owner of a neighborhood tavern was in the back room playing pinochle. The bartender came up to him and said, "Is Maloney good for a couple of drinks?"

The owner, without looking up from his cards, asked, "Has he had 'em?"

"He has."

"He is!"

After a three-day drinking bout, Tooley and Bragan registered at a hotel and asked for twin beds. However, in the darkness they both got into the same bed. "Hey," yelled Tooley, "I think a homo has crept in bed with me."

"There's a queer in my bed, too," called Bragan.

"Let's throw the fairies out," called back the first.

A terrific wrestling match ensued and finally Tooley went sailing out of the bed. "How'd you make out?" he called from the floor.

"I threw my guy out," said the other Irishman. "How about you?"

"He threw me out."

"Well that makes us even. Get into bed with me."

What's the official animal of Ireland?
The booze hound.

There was an Irishman named Sydney,
Who drank till he ruined his kidney.
   It shriveled and shrank,
   As he sat there and drank,
But he'd had a good time at it, didn't he?

The Irishman was taking an aptitude test. Most of the simple questions had him chewing on his pencil and squirming in the chair. But glancing down the printed sheet, he came to one query that gave him no trouble at all.

"Who do you consider the greatest Americans in history?" the paper read.

Without the slightest hesitation, the Irishman printed in the space provided, "Tom Collins and Johnnie Walker."

Irish Rheumatism: A disease whose victims get stiff in all the joints; sometimes known as alcoholics' arthritis

Rafferty reeled down the street and bumped into a middle-aged lady. As he thickly apologized she reprimanded him, "Don't you know drinking will ruin your stomach?"

"So what?" the Irishman hicked, "I'll keep my coat buttoned."

Mrs. Keegan entered an elevator at the 23rd floor. It was the operator, McCann's first day on the job.

He dropped through space at a dizzy speed, then threw on the brake and brought the car to a shuddering halt.

"Did I stop too quick?" asked McCann.

"Oh, no, indeed!" said Mrs. Keegan from the rear of the car. "I always wear me bloomers down around me ankles."

A loud-mouthed drunk stood at a bar and yelled, "Show me an Irishman and I'll show you a fool!"

McCoy, a giant of a man, stepped up to the loudmouth and said, "I'm an Irishman."

The loudmouth gulped in fear and said, "And I'm a fool."

How do you make an Irish Stew?

Keep him in whiskey for 20 years.

Mrs. Hatton wanted to scare her husband out of his terrible drinking habit. One night she dressed up like the devil and waited for him in an alley.

Soon the bar closed for the night and Hatton staggered toward home, Mrs. Hatton jumped out at him and yelled, "Yaaa! I'm the devil!"

Hatton held out his hand and said, "How da' ya' do, I married your sister!"

Judge: What induced you to steal this case of whiskey?

Cleary: I was hungry.

Sullivan walked into a saloon and ordered a glass of beer. "Say," he called out to the bartender, "how many kegs of beer do you use up every day?"

"Five," answered the barkeep. "Why'd you ask?"

"If I can show you how you can sell twice as much beer, will you buy me a drink?"

"Sure thing," agreed the bartender. "How can I sell twice as much beer each day?"

"Easy!" said Sullivan. "Fill up the glasses!"

"Uncle fell down the stairs with two quarts of liquor."

"Did he spill it?"

"No, he kept his mouth shut."

Sergeant Clancy was putting a squad of recruits through their drill. Try as he would he couldn't get a straight line. Finally in exasperation, he shouted, "What's the matter with ye? Can't ye line up? That line is as crooked as a corkscrew. All of ye fall out and take a look at it."

Irish Diplomacy: The ability to tell a man to go to hell so that he will look forward to making the trip

"O'Reilly is the most insecure man I've ever known!"
    "Why do you say that?"
    "When he goes to confession he always takes along his lawyer."

"You say Shaunessy's got a split personality?"
    "Yeah. One side of him likes scotch, rye, bourbon, gin and pretzels."
    "Well?"
    "Then there's the other side of him that doesn't like pretzels!"

SIGN IN TOOHEY'S TAVERN
NEVER DRINK WHILE DRIVING —
YOU MIGHT HIT A BUMP AND SPILL SOME

Reardon rushed into the neighborhood tavern. "Quick, bartender," he shouted, "give me three whiskies before the trouble starts!"
    The bartender jumped to the order and Reardon downed the three drinks in quick succession.
    "Now," said the bartender, "what's the trouble? When does it start?"
    "Right now," replied Reardon, "I haven't got a penny in my pockets."

Shebang: An Irish girl who can't say no

Fogarty began to drop in at Barney's Bar regularly, and his order was always the same—two martinis. After several weeks of this, Barney asked him why he didn't order a double instead.

"It's a sentimental thing," said Fogarty, "A very dear friend of mine died a few weeks ago, and before his death he asked that when I drink I have one for him, too."

A week later Fogarty came in and ordered one martini.

"What about your dead buddy? Why only one martini today?"

"This is my buddy's drink," came the reply. "I'm on the wagon."

Sean made his way unsteadily along the office corridor. He looked intently at the letters on the glass door and, with narrowed eyes, turned the handle and walked in.

"Ish thish Alcoholicks Anonymush?" he lisped.

"Yes, sir! D'you wish to join?"

"No—to reshign."

There was a young coleen named Flynn
Who thought fornication a sin,
But when she was tight,
It seemed quite all right;
So everyone filled her with gin.

Kelly had just fallen into a ditch. His friend Brady came along and shouted down, "Kelly, my friend, are you killed? Come on, if you're killed, speak up and say so."

"I'm alive, called back Kelly. "It's just that I've had the speech knocked out of me and I can't answer you."

116

Denny drained the last glass at the bar and said to his friend, "Paddy, tell me, where did I leave my coat?"

"Sure, you've got it on you," said Paddy.

"Ah, it's a good thing you told me, else I'd gone home without it."

"What a terrible electric storm we had last night," said Mrs. McCormick at breakfast.

"Then why didn't you wake me up?" demanded Mr. McCormick. "You know I can't sleep during thunder and lightning."

Salesman Milarkey was trying to sell some iron window sashes. "These sashes'll last you *forever*," he said to the customer. "And afterwards, when they are worn out, you can sell them for old iron."

Judge Foley pounding for order at a trial, shouted, "We want nothing but silence, and very little of that!"

"All right, McQuinnlan," said the Judge, "you've been brought here for drinking!"

"Well, your Honor," said McQuinnlan. "What are we waitin' for—let's get started!"

"A man who'd maliciously set fire to a barn, and burn up a stable of horses and mules," declared Judge Lynch to the jury, "ought to be kicked to death by a jackass— and I'd like to be the one to do it!"

The Irish lover was overheard to say, "It's a great comfort to be alone, especially when yer sweetheart is with ye."

Sweeney and Phelps were discussing architecture. "Modern buildings are more beautiful than old ones," declared Sweeney.

"An' will ye show me," insisted Phelps, "any new building that has lasted as long as the ancient ones?"

"Your money or your life!" cried the bandit.

"You go ahead and take me life," said Shannahan. "I'm saving my money for me old age."

The chairman of a company in Ireland said at the annual meeting of directors and shareholders, "It is alleged that half of our directors do the work while the other half do nothing at all. I assure you, gentlemen, that the reverse is the case."

BUMPER STICKER
IRISHMEN KNOW THE POWER OF
POSITIVE DRINKING

Phil Donahue, the master television host, told this titillator at the Vince Lombardi Golf Classic banquet:

Clusky went to a confession for the first time in twenty-five years. "Tell me," asked the priest. "Did you ever sleep with a woman?"

"Eh, no, Father," replied Clusky.

"Now, son," said the priest, "I'll ask you again. Did you ever sleep with a woman?"

"Ah, ey, ah, no, Father!"

"There's just you and me and God listening. I'm going to ask you once more. In the last twenty-five years have you ever slept with a woman?"

"Well, eh, come to think of it, Father," said Clusky, "I did doze off a time or two!"

Mrs. Brady was passing over the border from Northern Ireland into Southern Ireland when a customs official stopped her. Reaching for a suspicious bulge under her coat he uncovered a bottle full of brown liquid.

"And what is this?" he asked.

"Why it's nothin' but some holy water," said Mrs. Brady.

The officer took a swig from the bottle and nearly choked. "Just as I thought, a hundred-proof Irish whiskey!"

"Saints be praised," replied the Irish woman. "Another miracle!"

McMaken returned from a visit to his family in Galway. "What kind of a state is Ireland in today?" asked his neighbor.

"Status quo!" replied McMaken. "In the south of Ireland we have the Catholics and in the north the Protestants, and they're at each other's throats as usual all the time. If only they were heathen so they could live together like good Christians."

Danny Thomas told this to an Italian audience at a testimonial dinner honoring Jimmy Durante:

Lanagan, aged eighty-eight, was on his death bed and Father Feeney was trying to administer the "final blessing."

"Open your eyes," said the Father, "we've got to save your immortal soul."

Lanagan opened one eye, closed it, and tried to doze off. He was having a nice sleep. "Come on now!" cried the priest. "If you don't want to go to confession, at least answer me this: Do you renounce the Devil and all his works?"

"Well, I don't know, Father," said Lanagan, opening his eyes. "At a time like this, it ain't smart to antagonize anybody!"

The lovesick Irish maiden wound up her prayers each night by saying, "And dear Lord, please have Murphy on me!"

The traffic accident was an everyday happening. The first car had stopped for a light and the second had plowed into it from behind.

The only odd circumstance was that the first vehicle was being driven by a minister and the second by a priest.

A policeman came over as the two clergymen began arguing with each other.

"How fast would you say he was going," interjected Officer O'Malley, "when he backed into you, Father?"

Walsh stumbled out of a saloon and into a church he thought was a cathedral, and fell asleep. The sexton soon woke him and told him they were closing. "They don't close cathedrals," said Walsh.

"This isn't a cathedral," said the sexton. "It's a Presbyterian church."

Walsh looked around and saw stained-glass windows of St. Luke, St. Mark, and St. Thomas.

"And since when," asked the Irishman, "did the saints become Presbyterians?"

Maureen was a very devout Catholic, so everybody was surprised when she married out of the faith. But true to her upbringing, Maureen went to church regularly.

One Sunday morning, she rose early as usual. She slipped out of her nightgown and started to get dressed. As she leaned back to hook her bra, she noticed that her husband was awake and watching her every move. The bedsheets were rising higher and higher as he watched. Maureen sighed, unhooked her bra, sat down on the bed and unclasped her garters, undressing completely.

"I thought you were going to church, honey," said her husband, "You haven't missed a Sunday."

"The Catholic church will stand forever," declared Maureen getting into the bed. "But how long can you trust a Presbyterian prick?"

McGinty sat in the confessional. "Father," he said to the priest, "I don't feel I need forgiveness for me various adulteries."

"Why not?" asked the astonished priest.

"Well," said McGinty, "the only married women I have relations with are Jewish!"

"Ah, you're right, me son!" said the priest. "That's the only way to screw the Jews!"

Kennedy came along the road to find his friend Harrigan lying in the ditch where he had been tossed by a ten-ton truck. As he lay on his back groaning the rain came pouring down and lightning flashed about him. "Kennedy, Kennedy—get me a rabbi. Get me a rabbi."

"Are you mad, Harrigan? Sure you're a Roman Catholic and what would you want a rabbi for?"

The victim opened his eyes reproachfully, "Arrah, Kennedy, you wouldn't think of asking a priest to come out on a night like this."

The Mother Superior of a convent was interviewing the three girls graduating from the high school.

"Well, Margaret," she asked the first, "what will you be doing when you leave us?"

"Oh, Mother," the girl replied, "I'm going to stay here and take the veil!"

"Bless you," said the nun. "And you Katherine, what are your plans?"

"Oh," replied the girl. "I am going to continue to get a good Catholic education and then teach little children in a parochial school."

"Wonderful," said the nun. "And what will you do, Eileen?"

"I'm going to be a prostitute," replied the girl.

The Mother Superior shrieked and fainted to the floor.

They quickly revived her, the nun gasped, "Eileen, say that again."

"I am going to be a prostitute!" said the girl.

"Oh, Saints preserve us!" said the nun, crossing herself quickly. "I thought you said a Protestant!"

On returning from his honeymoon, Michael phoned his father at the office.

"Good to hear from you, son. Tell me, how's married life?"

"Dad, I'm really upset. I think I married a nun."

"A nun?" asked the startled father. "What do you mean?"

"Oh, you know, Dad, none in the morning and none at night."

"Oh, that," groaned the older man. "Come for dinner Saturday and I'll introduce you to the Mother Superior!"

Sisters Maria Theresa and Mary Elizabeth were walking down a street when they were grabbed by two men, dragged into an alley, and raped.

Twenty minutes later, the nuns continued their stroll. "What's Father going to say," said Sister Maria Theresa, "when we tell him we've been raped twice!"

"What do you mean twice?" asked her companion.

"We're coming back this way, aren't we?"

The little boy had been sitting close to the confession box door for a long time before Father Casey noticed him.

"Have you been listening to confessions all evening?" thundered the priest.

"Oh, no, Father. I'm only here since the woman who slept with the sailor came out."

Father Corrigan was hearing confession one Saturday evening when young Molly came in. "I've been away in another city for the past two years," she explained, "studying acrobatics. May I show you what I learned?"

"By all means," said the priest. Molly proceeded to do a complicated series of back flips and pinwheels, ending by standing on her head.

Just then Mrs. Carey and Mrs. Cassidy entered the church. "Glory be!" gasped Mrs. Carey. "Would yez look at what the good Father is giving for penance today—and me with old torn bloomers on!"

Mrs. MacNally was a new bride, and she wanted to be very certain that she was performing everything properly in her new life style.

One morning in the confession booth, she whispered to the parish priest, "Father, is it all right to have intercourse just before receiving communion?"

"Certainly, my child," replied the priest, "Just so long as you don't block the aisle!"

Mrs. Keen and Mrs. Monahan were sitting on their stoop watching the apartment across the street, which was rented by a young Italian girl. As a steady stream of men entered and left at half-hour intervals they keep saying, "She's a slut, . . ." "She's no good . . ." "She's a disgrace to the neighborhood."

Then after ten visitors, Father Gilhooley, the neighborhood priest, went in. "Oh, my," said Mrs. Keen, "the poor girl must be sick."

Faith, I've the luck O' the Irish,
It's the queerest tale e'er told,
I can take an item considered junk,
And turn the stuff into gold.

Begorrah, I once bought a washed-out nag,
From a scheming young chap named Herbie,
He laughed 'cause he thought he had me rooked,
But the old nag just won the Derby!

This very same Herbie sold me a swamp,
How he cackled as he took my coin,
But I quietly had the swamp graded,
It's known today as Des Moines.

Yes, I've got the luck of the Irish,
I'm a happy-go-lucky scalpeen,
With the flashing smile of Erin,
And the name of Irving Levine!

ITALIAN

"Hallo, TWA Airlines," said Manelli over the phone, "how long-a it takes to fly-a to Roma?"

"Just a minute," said the reservation clerk.

"Thank-a you so much!" said Manelli, and hung up.

What is the first lesson you receive at an Italian driving school?

How to open a locked car with a bent hanger.

"Hey, Vito, how'd your sister Angelina get that black eye?"

"She was jumping rope and forgot to put on her bra!"

Dalton was cleaning out the desk drawer in his den when he found a redemption check for shoes he had left for repair over twenty years ago. As a gag he went back to Banzini's Repair Shop and presented the check to the owner.

"I know it's over twenty years," he said "but maybe you'll be able to find them."

The old Italian took the receipt, wa¹ :d to the back of the store and returned in a few   nutes. "Okay, Mister," said Banzini, "I gotta da shoes. Come back-a Thursday, they be ready four o'clock."

Chinese-Italian Restaurant: Ah Fong Goo's

"Is it true all Italians are gangsters?"
"Don't be stupid! I say all Italians are lovers. Take Al Capone. You think he ever forgot Valentine's Day?"

How do Italians count money?
One, two, three, four, five, another, another, another. . . .

What do Italians call Canada?
Upper U.S.

What do they call Alaska?
Way Upper U.S.

A Mafioso chieftan wished to move into the higher levels of society but was afraid his girlfriend Roxie would embarrass him with her unpolished language. He decided to send her away for a very expensive crash course in grammar. Roxie returned three months later, burst into his office, and exclaimed, "Were you blue while I was gone?"

"All that money," cried the mobster, "and she still has her tenses wrong."

What is the national bird of Italy?
The stool pigeon.

Sometime during the year 1500, legend has it, a young
girl in Milan beseeched a famous artist she knew to
paint her portrait.
"I'm far too busy," he is supposed to have told her.
"Why not ask that fellow Da Vinci across the court-
yard, Mona? He needs the business!"

Bigamist: A fog over Italy

Why won't there ever be an Italian first lady in the
White House?
Because they'll never find enough plastic slipcovers
for all the furniture.

Bigotry: An Italian redwood

What's the difference between a monkey and an Italian?
The Italian has more fleas.

When Greek meets Greek they open a restaurant.
When Italian meets Italian—they rob it!

A sociologist was taking a survey based on the sexual
proclivities of various national and ethnic groups. He
approached an elderly Italian gentleman in a black suit
and, after the usual preliminaries, asked him how often
he had sexual intercourse.
"Oh, maybe ten, twelve times a year," stated the
old fellow.
"But you are Italian and Italians are supposed to
be very sexy," came the response.
"Listen, I don't think that is so bad for a sixty-
year-old priest who doesn't own a car."

Italian Girdle: A venetian bind

What does the government do with old garbage scows?
It sells them to Italians for houseboats.

Which bird is as sacred to Italians as the cow is to
Indians?
The guinea hen.

Why are rectal thermometers banned in Italy?
They cause too much brain damage.

The Italian surgeon was scrubbing up after the operation.
"Well, Dr. Picatelli, how did Mrs. Agnielli's
appendectomy go?" asked one of the interns.
"Appendectomy?" shrieked Picatelli. "I thought it
was an autopsy!"

Columbus Day: The Italian Yom Kippur

Muzzo had migrated to America and now he stood
before the Judge to find out whether he would get his
citizenship papers.
"Your Honor," said the frightened Italian; "I no
speak-a too good-a Hingleesh 'cause I no be in this-a
country too long-a time. Since-a I talk-a like thees, you
think-a I'm-a no getta my papers?"
The Judge said, "Donjoo worry, you gonna get-a
you papers!"

The whole Mafia is talking about the gangster's moll
who walked out on her boyfriend when she found out
he was just a finger man.

Why do Mafia hit men never indulge in sexual foreplay?
They're afraid of injuring their trigger fingers.

What is the first thing they do at Italian weddings after the priest says, "With this ring I thee wed"?
They take the handcuffs off the groom.

What are the three times an Italian sees his priest?
When he is born!
When he is married!
And when he is electrocuted!

Venzetti walked into a Fifth Avenue bank.
"Pardon me-a, I like-a to talk with the fella what arranges the loans."
"I'm sorry," said the guard, "but the loan arranger is out to lunch!"
"In dat-a case," said the Italian, "let me talk-a to Tonto!"

What is the main difference between Italian movie starlets and French movie starlets?
French starlets don't have hair on their chests.

Facenda and Satta met in the park:
"Hey, Satta, you make-a lots-a money now?"
"Yeah, I ain't-a doin' too bad!"
"What-a you gonna do with all-a you money?"
"I'm gonna do something I wanna do my whole-a life."
"What's-a that?"
"I'm-a gonna get me a Polack gardener."

What did the Italian girl say as she was being raped in a rented car?
"It's-a hurts!"

Villiani and Di Lucca were watching a jet fly overhead.
"Hey, atsa the Pope up there!" shouted Villiani.

"How you know dat?" asked Di Lucca.

"Atsa easy," replied the first Italian. "The airplane-a say TWA. Topa Wop Aboard."

Vice Versa: Dirty poetry from Italy

The priest stood before a hushed crowd of attentive villagers, and spoke to them. "You must not use-a the Pill!"

A lovely signorina stepped forward and said, "Look, you no play-a da game, you no make-a da rules!"

Father Ferrucio and Father Messina were sitting in a grotto chatting.

"Do you think the Pope will ever allow priests to marry?" asked Father Ferrucio.

"It won't happen in our time," replied Father Messina. "Maybe in our children's!"

An Italian painter named Giotto
Seduced a nun in a grotto
  The result of his crime
  Was two boys at one time.
"Give your sons to the church," was his motto.

The Pope was reading in his Vatican sanctuary when suddenly he was called to the telephone.

"This is a Father Novelli in New York," said the voice. "Your Holiness, I think that Jesus Christ is walking down the middle of Fifth Avenue. What should I do?"

"Look-a busy!" replied the Pontiff.

Operetta: A girl who works for the phone company

Fabrini and Giampa were passing time after their hero-sandwich lunch. "Hey," said Fabrini, "Did you know it took Michaelangelo more than twenty years to paint the dome of the Sistine Chapel?"

"Yeah?" said Giampa, "Well, he'd-a done it a lot faster if he'd-a got himself a paint roller!"

Michaelangelo was painting the ceiling of the Sistine Chapel. He was getting tired lying on his back and in rolling over noticed that a woman was praying down in the Chapel. The great artist decided to play a little prank.

He sat at the edge of the scaffold and shouted, "I am Jesus Christ! I am Jesus Christ! Listen to me and I will perform miracles!"

The Italian lady looked up clasping her rosary and answered back: "Shut up-a your mouth! I'm-a talk-a to your mother!"

What's the Italian word for refrigerator?
Ice-a box.

What's the Italian word for woman?
Nice-a box.

Innuendo: An Italian suppository

At the Frontier Hotel in Las Vegas, Comedian Dave Barry breaks up his audiences with these two beauts:

"If you want to learn to speak Italian," says Dave, "All you need to know is one word: Atsa.
Like, "Ats-a table! Ats-a chair! . . ."

131

McClanahan and Finzetti were digging a ditch. "My brotha just-a had-a twins!" exclained the recent arrival from Calabria. "A boy and a girl!"

"Now that's nice to hear," replied the son of Erin. "What did they call the girl?"

"Denise!" answered Finzetti.

"And what about the boy?" asked the Irishman.

"De Nephew!" said the Italian proudly.

Did you hear about the Italian girl who was so ugly garlic backed away from her?

What is the difference between an Italian mother-in-law and an elephant?

About fifty pounds.

Lupo and Rovelli were torpedoed during World War II. They managed to save themselves on a life raft.

Suddenly, Rovelli noticed a periscope skimming the water. He nudged his comrade and said, "Hey, is that a U-Boat?"

"No!" said Lupo seeing the periscope. "That's-a no my boat!"

What do they call an Italian submarine captain?

Chicken of the sea.

What's the easiest way to spot an Italian ship?

When it's put on water — it sinks.

Why was the Italian navy so useless during the war?

The cannons were too heavy and all three garbage scows sank.

What is the first tactical training given to Italian army recruits?

How to retreat.

D'Angelo, the immigrant, had to travel by train from New York to Raleigh, North Carolina. When he was met by a cousin it was obvious that D'Angelo was in a very bad mood.

"What happened?" asked his relative.

"Ah, that goddamn-a conductor he tell-a me no do this and no do that!" exclaimed the Italian. "I take out-a my sand-a-wich and he say, 'No—inna dining car.' I starta- drink-a some vino and he say, 'No—inna club-a car.' So I go inna club-a car, meet-a girl, and she take-a me back to her empty compartment and then the goddamn conductor he come along ana yell, "No'foka, Virginia, no'foka Virginia!'"

What is the thinnest book in the World?

THE LIST OF ITALIAN WAR HEROES.

What do you get if you cross a retarded Puerto Rican with a baboon?

An Italian intellectual.

Opera: Italian Vaudeville

A reporter approached Signora Delarosa backstage at the San Francisco Opera House. "Tell me," he asked, "How do you manage to hold that high C for so long?"

"I hold it," said the soprano, "as long as the stage manager keeps sticking pins in my ass!"

Enrico Caruso was the matinee idol of the society opera world in the early 1900's. He was also privately one of the more active lovers of his time. The following remark is attributed to the great Italian tenor:

"I never make love in the morning," Caruso is supposed to have said. "It's bad for the voice; it's bad for the health; and, besides, you never know who you might meet in the afternoon."

Three weeks after arriving in America Mario telephoned his mother in Rome.

"*Mama mia!*" he bellowed excitedly. "I'm-a so happy. I'm-a gonna marry an Americana girl!"

"No! No!" pleaded his mother. "American girl-a no good. She's a bad cook. She's a bad in-a da bed. And if you have-a da fight, she's gonna call you a wop!"

Despite his mother's please Mario married the girl and a month later phoned her again.

"Mama! Mama! You all-a wrong!" said Mario. "She's a great cook! She's-a wonderful in-a the bed! And Mama, the only time she's-a call me a wop is when I call-a her a coon!"

Columbus was the first wheeler dealer. He didn't know where he was going. When he got there he didn't know where he was. When he got back he didn't know where he had been. And he did it all on borrowed money.

After the marriage ceremony of her only daughter, Mrs. Fazio took the girl aside and gave her advice about the first night.

"What-a happens in-a the bedroom is-a very important," said the mother. "Tonight, you put-a on a lots-a perfume. Sprinkle a powder on-a the bed. Wear a real-a flimsy nightagown. You be ready when you man comes to get-a you!"

"Mama!" said the girl. "I know how to screw, but how do you make lasagna!"

At an Italian wedding how can you tell the difference between members of the Mafia and the musicians?

The musicians are the ones without the violin cases.

Do you know why Polish jokes are so short?

So Italians can understand them.

Eagan and Johansen were standing on a street corner. "I can't stand Eyetalians," said Eagan. "I hate 'em! They turn my stomach!"

Just then an organ grinder and his monkey came by. The angry Irishman gave the monkey a quarter.

"Why'd you do that?" asked Johansen. "I thought you hated Italians!"

"True," said Eagan, "but they're so cute when they're little!"

As an experiment, two scientists decided to mate a male human with a female gorilla. They agreed only someone really stupid would submit to such an act. So they went down to the docks and grabbed Fanelli who had just gotten off the boat.

"We'll give you five thousand dollars to go to bed with a gorilla!" proposed one of the scientists. "Will you do it?"

"Okay, I do it!" agreed Fanelli. "But on three conditions!"

"What are they?" asked the men of science.

"Firsta, I'm-a only gonna do it-a once!" said the Italian. "Second-a, nobody canna watch. And-a third, if a kid is born, it's-a gotta be raised a Catholic!"

Italian Diaphragm: A wop stopper

Did you hear about the Italian girl who ran out of wool while knitting a sweater so she finished it with spaghetti?

The first time she wore it, two meatballs followed her home.

At a Mafia party how can you tell the guest of honor?

He's the one with the brand-new cement overcoat.

On a road eight miles from Rome, Feldman, an American motorist, was stopped by a masked man who, brandishing a revolver, demanded in a thick Sicilian accent that he get out of the car.

Feldman obeyed, pleading, "Take my money, my car, but don't kill me!"

"I no kill-a you," replied the Italian, "if you do what I say." Whereupon, he told the tourist to unzip his pants and masturbate. Though shocked, the American did what he was told.

"Good," said the masked stranger. "Now-a do it again." Feldman protested, but the gun was menacingly waved, so, with extreme difficulty, he repeated the act.

"Again," commanded the Sicilian, "or I kill-a you!" Summoning superhuman resources, the exhausted motorist relieved himself yet a third time.

Suddenly, the Italian gave an order and a beautiful young brunette stepped from behind the rocks. "Now," said the highwayman, "you can give-a my sister a ride into town!"

JAPANESE

Have you heard that the leading manufacturer of imported vibrators is a Japanese firm that now calls itself Genital Electric?

Sakanooki: Japanese word for bloomers

In Tokyo, a huge and ferocious sumo wrestler won the Most Vicious Man in the World trophy, and, as a sort of bonus, his manager fixed him up for the night with an unusually attractive geisha girl.

When the girl went to the manager's office the next morning to collect her stipend, she was in a bad mood. "Whoever told that ape he could screw?" she snapped.

The manager shrugged. "Who's going to tell him he can't?"

> The ladies who live in Japan
> Exist just for pleasing a man.
> They'll give him fellatio
> Or a lay on the patio
> Or even a goose with a fan.

Did you hear about the guy who was half-Japanese and half-Black?

Every December 7 he attacks Pearl Bailey.

Comedian Pat Morita tells about the Japanese General who called his men together on a small Pacific island during World War II.

"Men," said the army officer, "I've got good news and bad news. First, the bad news. There is nothing left to eat on the island except sea gull droppings. Now the good news. There isn't enough to go around."

Japansie: An Oriental homo

Foster, in Tokyo on business, knew no Japanese. Even so, he pursuaded an attractive girl who spoke no English to come to his hotel room.

All during their lovemaking, the Oriental kept shouting, *"Nachagai ana!"* with great feeling. Foster felt proud that he could get the girl so aroused to keep yelling, *"Nachagai ana!"*

The next afternoon, he played golf with a Japanese industrial tycoon. When the Oriental made a hole-in-one, Foster, attempting to make a good impression, exclaimed, *"Nachagai ana! Nachagai ana!"*

"What do you mean," snapped the tycoon, "the wrong hole?"

American: Isn't it wonderful how your people admire the United States?

Japanese: It is true. To us it's the world's largest Datsun dealership.

What is the official animal of Japan?
  The camera bug.

Lackanooki: A dread disease among Japanese

A downtown store featured a plaque in its window
reading
  BUY AMERICAN
Printed in small letters at the bottom was
  MADE IN JAPAN

What's Japanese for leg joint?
  Nippon-knees.
What's Japanese for breasts?
  Nippon-these!

Did you hear about the little boy whose family was so
poor, he wasn't born—he was made in Japan?

Once, a great tournament was held in feudal Japan to
select the best samurai swordsman. After exhaustive
eliminations, three finalists remained. Each was given a
small box with a fly in it. The first warrior released the
fly and then divided it cleanly in half in flight.
  The second was even more skillful, slicing his fly
into quarters with two lightning like strokes of his keen
blade.
  Then came the third samurai's turn. He released
his fly and swung his sword, but the fly kept on flying.
"Ah," said the judge, "your fly has escaped unharmed."
  "He still flies," countered the proud warrior, "but
he will no longer reproduce."

Most things we buy say MADE IN JAPAN
  I think we're getting the needle.
Last night I purchased some Spanish Fly;
  It was ground-up Japanese beetle.

Nooki Looki: A pelvic examination in Japan

A sailor named Harry had an affair with a geisha girl and then he came back to the states. Soon after he received a letter from her:

"Dear Harry: You gone three months, me gone three months—should I carry Harry or hari-kari?"

Did you hear about the Japanese call girl who went broke because no one had a yen for her?

There was a young miss from Japan
Who danced on the stage with a fan.
    Then came a day
    When the fan blew away,
And damned if it wasn't a man!

It is common knowledge that the Japanese have made large investments in the United States. They have been very quietly buying up many industries and businesses. Now there's word that they have just bought Forest Lawn Cemetery in California.

They're going to change the name to "Jap in the Box."

Japanese Cunnilingus: Constluctive cliticism

Did you hear about the new Japanese camera on the market?

When you trip the shutter, it goes *crick!*

Zimmerman, on a business trip to Tokyo, was having lunch with a Japanese friend.

"You Americans don't know how to make love," said the Oriental. "In Japan we go to bed with wife, begin to make love, after few minute we stop, get up for cup of hot tea. Then go back to bed, make love for ten minute, then get up and have bowl of rice. Then make love some more, get up take bath together, then we finally finish the act."

Two weeks later, back in Brooklyn, Zimmerman got into bed with his wife and began making love to her, suddenly he stopped and said, "Let's have a glass of tea."

"Are you crazy?" she said.

"Come on," he insisted. Soon they were back in bed and a little while, he stopped and said, "Now we're gonna have a pastrami sandwich."

"Are you nuts?" exclaimed his spouse.

They got back into bed and after a few minutes Zimmerman said, "Now we're gonna take a bath together."

When they finished, the Jewish couple went back to the bedroom and wound up their love making.

"Well," asked Zimmerman, "what did you think of that?"

"Wonderful," replied his wife, "but where did you learn to screw like a Jap?"

JEWISH

Manny ran into Arnold, an old friend who unfortunately stuttered very badly. "Where have you been, Arnold," asked Manny.

"I j-j-just went d-d-down for a j-j-job at the r-r-radio station as an-n-n-nouncer," stuttered Arnold.

"How did you make out?" asked Manny.

"Okay," said Arnold, "b-but they d-d-don't hire J-J-J-Jews."

Two men are walking in the city. The first one says, "I've never seen so many Chinese restaurants in one area before!"

"Naturally," replied his friend, "this is a Jewish neighborhood."

Gilligan, Frizzoli, and Lieberman were telling how they were mistaken for great men.

The Irishman said, "I was walking along the street and a fella yelled, "Hello, St. Patrick!"

The Italian said, "That's nothing, I was standing on a corner, a man passed me and said, "Hello, Mussolini."

"That's nothing," said the Jew. "As I walked across the park this morning a policeman yelled at me, " 'Jesus Christ, get off the grass!' "

While at a synagoge dance Lupowitz lost a wallet containing $600. He went up to the microphone and announced, "Gentlemen, I lost my wallet with six hundred dollars in it. To the man that finds it I will give fifty dollars."

A voice yelled from the rear, "I'll give seventy-five."

David came from an Orthodox family. One day he announced, "Mama, I'm going to marry an Irish girl named Maggie Coyle!"

The woman froze in shock.

"That's nice, David," she said. "But don't tell your papa. You know he's got a weak heart.

"And I wouldn't tell your sister, Ida. Remember how strongly she feels about religious questions.

"And don't mention it to your brother, Louis, he might give you a bust in the mouth.

"Me, it's all right, you told. I'm gonna commit suicide anyway."

Fishman was dying and his children gathered at his bedside. The eldest, Rubie, spoke in hushed tones, "Papa, tell us, where would you like to be buried—here in Los Angeles, or back in New York?"

Fishman opened his eyes slightly and said, "Surprise me."

Feingold immigrated to America and after many years of hard work became a very wealthy man. Now on his deathbed, with his wife, Sarah, standing by, he started to dispose of his worldly possessions.

"My Cadillac with the push-button-motorcycle-cop-detector I leave to my son, Sam."

"Better you should leave it to Joe," said his wife. "He's a better driver."

"All right," he whispered. "My Rolls Royce I bequeath to my daughter Linda."

"You better give it to your nephew, Willie," Sarah interrupted. "He's a very conservative driver."

"All right, give it to Willie. My twelve-cylinder Jaguar I give to my niece, Sally."

"Personally, I think Judy should get it."

Feingold raised his head and shouted, "Sarah, please, who's dying? You or me?"

Old man Bernstein lay dying. The entire family had gathered around the deathbed. In a soft feeble voice, he inquired, "Is Sol here?"

"Yes, Papa," said his eldest son.

"Is Lester here?"

"Yes, Dad!" answered the boy.

"Is Eli here?"

"I'm right here!" said the youngest son.

"If you're all here," said Bernstein, "who's minding the store?"

On the lower east side of New York stood Plotkin's Pickle Stand. Mrs. Solomon walked over to the barrel, pulled out a pickle, had Plotkin weigh it, then asked: "How much?"

"Fifteen cents!" he replied.

Several times she pulled out pickles; on each occasion had the owner weigh it only to tell her it was fifteen cents. "Look lady," he said, "it's a pickle! It ain't a putz. It don't get bigger and it don't get smaller. The price is fifteen cents."

144

Business partners Slutsky and Gross were fishing in a
small rowboat on a lake in the Catskills. Suddenly, a
storm came up, the boat capsized, and, while Slutsky
began to swim, Gross floundered and sputtered
helplessly. He was sinking.

"Say," said Slutsky, swimming away, "can you
float alone?"

"I'm drowning," sputtered Gross, "and he's talkin'
business!"

Cantor, Klein, Levy, and Strulowitz met for lunch.
After ordering, Cantor said "Oy, Oy, Oy!"

"Ay, ay, ay!" answered Klein.

"Yai, Yai, Yai!" added Levy.

"Look," said Strulowitz, "if you fellas are gonna
talk business, I ain't gonna stay!"

A teacher said to her class, "Who was the greatest man
who ever lived? The pupil who answers this question
will receive this large apple!"

A little Italian boy raised his hand and said,
"Columbus."

Then an Irish kid said, "St. Patrick."

The Epstein boy, lifted his hand and said, "Jesus
Christ!"

The teacher was amazed. She called him to her
desk, handed him the apple, and asked, "Sheldon, you
don't believe in Jesus as the Christ, so why did you say
he was the greatest man who ever lived?"

"Actually," said Sheldon, "I think Moses was a
much greater man, but business is business!"

The young son of a garment maker was in school one
day when the teacher asked him to name the four
seasons.

"I only know two," said the boy. "Busy and slack!"

A jewelry store on Fifth Avenue bore the gold-engraved letters, s. ASTOR. Seeing the sign, a bejeweled matron thought to herself, "I wonder if they are *the* Astors." So she went inside.

"Pardon me, sir," she asked the proprietor, "but are you the Boston Astors?"

"No," he replied, politely. "The Boston Astors are the Steinbergs; we're the Ecksteins!"

Benny had just begun helping his father out in their small clothing store. A customer came in with a question that sent him to the back of the store.

"Hey, Pop," asked Benny, "the customer wants to know if those all-wool unshrinkable shirts will shrink?"

"Does it fit him?" asked the father.

"No," said Benny, "it's too large."

"Well, then," said the father, "tell him it'll shrink."

Arlene, a high-class hooker, refused to sleep with Mendelbaum because she hated Jews. He finally prevailed upon her to accept him for $200 for one night. "Okay," she agreed, "but only if you make love to me silently in the pitch-dark, so I don't have to see your damned hook nose."

He agreed, and, that night, amazed her by making love to her fifteen times in a row, stopping only to go to the bathroom between each bout.

"My god, Mendelbaum," she said finally, "I never imagined you were so virile!"

"Ah ain't Mendelbaum, ma'am," said a black man's voice, "Mendelbaum is downstairs selling tickets."

Edelstein owned a little sandwich shop delicatessen on the lower east side of New York. He was called down to the Internal Revenue for tax examination.

"I don't understand," said the revenue agent. "You have a small store where you sell mostly sandwiches and coffee, and on your tax return you charge twelve trips to Israel as a business expense."

"Oh, that!" said Edelstein. "We also deliver!"

One September morning after Labor Day, Levin and
Ostrow met for lunch. They hadn't seen each other for
several months.

"I have just lived through a summer I never
thought I would see," said Levin. "June was a disaster.
Never have I seen a June like that. When July came, I
realized that June was terrific, because with July I went
right into the cellar. July was so bad—. . ."

"For heaven's sake," interrupted Ostrow, "why're
you coming to me with these piddling matters? You
wanna hear *real* trouble, I got it. Yesterday my only son
came home, told me he's gonna marry another fella.
My boy is a homosexual! What could be worse than
that?"

"I'll tell you," said Levin, "August!"

After discussing the weather, family, and related
subjects, one of two dress industrialists who met on
Broadway said, "How come you don't ask me how
business is?"

"All right, how's business?"

"Don't ask!"

Rosenfeld, a New York men's clothing manufacturer,
was returning to America after a business trip to Israel.
On the way back, he decided to stop off in Rome and
take in the sights. Two weeks later, he finally arrived
home.

"How was the trip?" asked his sales manager.

"Fantastic!" replied Rosenfeld. "In Israel I sold a
thousand more suits than any of us expected. Then I
stopped off in Rome and saw all the historical sights. I
got in with a sight-seeing group and we had an audience
with the Pope."

"The Pope himself? You don't say!" exclaimed the
sales manager. "What does he look like?"

"Oh," said Rosenfeld, "I'd say about a 44 short."

Lou Jacobi, the fine comedy character actor, tells about Garfinkel, the garment manufacturer, who has spent his entire life tending to business. He worked hard for forty years and now, finally, he had the kind of money that would allow him to buy or do whatever he wanted.

One morning, Garfinkel sent for his messenger boy. "I want you to get me five pounds of marijuana," he shouted. "I also want a broad that'll go three ways. Then get me a seven-foot hooker with black boots and a whip."

The messenger left and returned in an hour. "I'm sorry, Mr. Garfinkel," he said, "I got the grass and the three-way broad but I can't find a seven-foot hustler with black boots and a whip."

"In that case," yelled Garfinkel, "cancel the order and get me a prune Danish!"

Customer: You said this shirt was all wool. Here I find a label sewed inside that says ALL COTTON.

Store Owner: Well, you see that label is sewed in there to scare the moths away!

Benson went to Krantz's Clothing Store to buy himself a suit. He found just the style he wanted, so he took the jacket off the hanger and tried it on.

Krantz came up to him. "Yes, sir. It looks wonderful on you."

"It may *look* wonderful," said Benson, "but it fits terrible. The shoulders pinch."

"Put on the pants," said Krantz. "They're so tight, you'll forget all about the shoulders!"

Freeman and Singer, two small dress manufacturers, were having an argument. Berman overheard the conversation and tapped Singer on the shoulder.

"Listen," he said, "I know you forty years and you ain't yet paid a bill. What're you trying to cut the price down for? Whatever it is, you know you ain't gonna pay it."

"Sure, I know," said Singer, "but Freeman is such a nice guy I wanna keep his losses down."

The reporter for the *Wall Street Journal* asked
Weintraub, the stockbroker, "What's the latest dope on
Wall Street?"

"My son," he answered.

Weinstein, a very wealthy businessman, had an
unattractive daughter. The truth is, she was ugly as
sin. But he found a young man to marry her and after
ten years they had two children.

Weinstein called his son-in-law into the office one
day. "Listen," he said, "you've given me two beautiful
grandchildren, you've made me very happy. I'm gonna
give you 49 percent of the business."

"Thank you, Pop!"

"Is there anything else I could do for you?"

"Yeah, buy me out!"

How can you tell a Jewish gangster from an Italian
gangster?

The Jew is the one wearing an Italian suit.

Jacobs went into Levine's clothing store to ask the
price of a suit on display in the window.

"You picked the best suit in the place," said
Levine, "and to show you that I like to do business
with a man who's got such good taste, I'm gonna make
you a special proposition. I wouldn't ask you one
hundred dollars for the suit. I wouldn't ask you ninety.
I wouldn't ask you seventy. Sixty dollars is the price
for you, my friend."

Jacobs replied, "I wouldn't give you sixty, and I
wouldn't give you fifty. My offer is forty.

"Sold," said Levine. "That's the way I like to do
business. No chiseling."

"Ethics," said Schoenfeld to his son, "is the most important thing in business."

"Why is that, Dad?" asked the boy.

"Take just today, for instance. A man came in and bought something, paid me with a hundred-dollar bill. After he left, I found that there's really two bills stuck together—the customer paid me two hundred dollars instead of one. And here's where business ethics comes in. The question is: Should I tell my partner or shouldn't I?"

Fogel and Rifkin, two garment industry moguls, were on the verge of bankruptcy. Suddenly, a West Coast outlet wanted to buy their whole line, at a price that would make the partners solvent again.

"I gotta have the deal approved by the home office," said the buyer. "I'm going back tomorrow. If you don't hear from me by Friday closing time, you can be sure everything's okay."

The week went by slowly; and Friday crawled. Fogel and Rifkin squirmed at their desks, unable to concentrate on work. Without this deal, they would definitely go under.

Two o'clock went by, three o'clock, then four o'clock, and now they were close to pay dirt. Four-thirty came, and suddenly, a messenger burst into the office. "Telegram!" he said. The men froze in terror.

Finally Fogel opened the telegram, read it quickly.

"Rifkin," he shrieked. "Good news! Your brother died!"

While waiting in the audience for the speaker at a public meeting, Weiss seemed very nervous. He glanced over his shoulder from time to time and shifted about in his seat. At last he arose and shouted, "Is there a Christian Scientist in the audience?"

A dignified woman three rows over stood up and said, "I am a Christian Scientist."

"Lady," said Weiss, "would you mind changing seats with me? I'm sitting in a draft."

Mrs. Zimmer hired an interior designer to have the house redecorated.

"All right," said the decorator, "how would you like it done? Modern?"

"Me, modern? No," said Mrs. Zimmer.

"How about French?"

"French? Where would I come to a French house?"

"Perhaps Italian provincial?"

"God forbid!"

"Well, madam, what period do you want?"

"What period? I want my friends to walk in, take one look, and drop dead! *Period!*"

"My name is Wellington S. Rabinowitz."

"What does the "S" stand for?"

"Nothing. My father dropped a noodle on my birth certificate."

Mrs. Brickman, aged eighty-nine, lived in a retirement center. Despite her age, the old woman still had a great spirit. "Tonight, Ida," she told another senior citizen, "for fun I'm gonna run through the dining room without my clothes on!"

"What?" shrieked her friend. "You gonna go naked in the dinner room?"

"That's right!"

That night—without a stitch of clothing on, ancient Mrs. Brickman dashed through the dining room. Two elderly men spotted her.

"Was that Mrs. Brickman?" asked one.

"Yeah," said the other. "And whatever she's wearing—she should have it pressed!"

Rosen had both legs broken in an accident. He sued for damages, alleging he was crippled and would have to spend all his life in a wheelchair. The insurance company doctor testified that the bones had healed, that Rosen was able to walk and that he was faking. However the judge took pity and awarded him $100,000 damages. Rosen was wheeled to the head office to collect his check.

"You're not getting away with this," said the manager. "We're going to watch you night and day. If we find you can walk, not only will you repay the damages, but you'll also be up for perjury. Here's the one hundred thousand dollars. What do you intend to do with it?"

"Me and my wife are gonna travel. We're starting out at Norway and going through Scandinavia, then Switzerland, Italy, Greece—and I don't care if your agents and spies are watching, I'll be in my wheelchair. Naturally we're going to Israel. From there we go across to France where we are going to visit a place called Lourdes, and there you're going to see some miracle."

A family by the name of Cohen living in Madrid, Spain, named their little girl Carmen. Her mother called her Carmen. But the father, who had wanted a boy badly, always called her by her last name, Cohen.

After awhile, the poor girl didn't know whether she was Carmen or Cohen.

Bagel: A doughnut dipped in cement

Groucho Marx was with his wife and daughter when they passed a beautiful hotel swimming pool. It was a very hot Sunday afternoon and they decided to take a dip. The manager said, "I'm sorry, but this place is restricted."

"That's okay," said Groucho, "I'm Jewish and my wife is Gentile. That makes my daughter half-Jewish. Do you mind if she goes in the water up to her waist?"

Sampson, the country fair sideshow strongman, grabbed a 500-pound barbell and lifted it above his head. He then kneeled under a piano on which heavy weights had been distributed and slowly raised the piano aloft.

The hawker then announced, "And now Sampson will take this ordinary lemon and using both hands will squeeze every bit of juice out of it. We'll pay five hundred dollars to anybody in this audience who can squeeze another drop of juice out of the lemon after Sampson has handled it."

Sampson took the lemon and crushed it into a pulpy mass. Then three powerful men from the crowd came up and each tried unsuccessfully to extrace a drop of juice out of the lemon.

The hawker asked, "Anyone else care to try?" A slight little man climbed up on the stage. He took the lemon, squeezed it, and out spouted a stream of juice.

The hawker paid the prize money and asked, "How did you get juice out of this lemon, where everyone else before had failed?"

"Well, you see, I've been a collector for the United Jewish Appeal for twelve years."

Mrs. Lipsky and Mrs. Fisch sat on the porch of a hotel in Lakewood.

"My watch stopped just before I came here so I took it back to Tiffany to be repaired," said Mrs. Lipsky. "If you'll be so kind, would you mind telling me what time it is on your watch?"

"Not at all!" said Mrs. Fisch, looking at her wrist. "It's exactly five rubies after seven diamonds!"

One of the ladies of the Sisterhood was talking excitedly about her wonderful trip to Israel.

"Did you go by chartered flight?" asked her friend. "No."

"By group flight?"

"No."

"Did you have an excursion rate?"

"The answer again was, "No."

"My God!" exclaimed the woman. "You mean you traveled retail?"

A whole bus load of women from the Hadassah and the United Jewish Appeal overturned on a Miami freeway and were killed. In Heaven, Saint Peter, without thinking, assigned them to hell. They had hardly been there a week, however, when Satan phoned Peter and demanded that he remove the women to heaven. They were a disrupting influence.

"Why, what have they done?" asked Peter.

"They have banded together, collected money, and employed engineers to install air-conditioning."

Mrs. Feinberg sat at the dining-room table in a Catskill hotel ready to order breakfast. "What would you like?" asked the waiter.

"I'll have some hot water with lemon. A dish of prunes. Then a large fig juice. A raw apple cut in little pieces over bran flakes. And a pot of coffee."

She then turned to the women at the next table and said, "You see? Nothing for *me*—everything for the bowels!"

Berkowitz met a beautiful brunette in Bermuda and tried to get her to fly home with him to New York.

"Come with me tonight and I'll buy you a mink coat," propositioned Berkowitz.

"I've got two minks hanging in my closet."

"A Buick convertible?"

"And what would I do with my Cadillac?"

"All right, I'll give you a stunning diamond bracelet."

She displayed the gems on her wrist. "Already have one—however, I'd be willing to consider a sizeable chunk of cash."

"Sorry," said Berkowitz, "that's the one thing I can't get wholesale!"

On Collins Avenue, Mrs. Baum complained of not feeling well. Her friend asked, "Have you been through the menopause yet?"

"With my stingy husband? I haven't even been through the Fontainebleau yet!"

Meyer: Did you get the check I sent you?
Isaacs: I got it twice—once from you and once from the bank.

Winkelman went to one of those Florida hotels where they feature a lot of exercise to keep you in trim, but Winkelman didn't want to exercise. "I came here to relax and rest, and that's what I'm gonna do."

He remained stubborn through his whole stay. As he was checking out, the manager said to him, "Before you leave, please do one exercise. To keep my record intact. Just bend down, keep your knees stiff, and touch your valise."

Winkelman agreed. He bent down, touched the valise and said, "What now?"

"Now," said the manager, "open the valise and give me back my towels."

Aronson of Aronson Fabrics answered the phone. A woman's voice said, "Do you mind calling my husband Jerome to the phone?"

"Jerome? Jerome?" asked Aronson. "Does he work for me?"

"Yes, he works for you," she replied. "But right now he's outside your store, picketing the place."

Israel is keeping pace with the modern world—even in the field of music. A new rock group just formed. They call themselves The Foreskins.

Brotsky was in Puerto Rico for a business convention. One night in front of his hotel, he was hailed seductively by a beautiful prostitute.

"Hallo, *Americano*," she said. "You wanna buy what I'm selling?"

Brotsky went with her. Ten days later, at home in New York, he found that he had caught gonorrhea.

The next year, in front of the same hotel, he was hailed by the same girl again.

"Hallo, *Americano*. You wanna buy what I'm selling?"

"Sure," he said. "What is it this time, cancer?"

What do you call an uncircumcised Jewish baby?
     A girl.

"Last night I went to see a Jewish porno movie, and it was quite an experience."

"What could a dirty Jewish movie be like?"

"It only lasted ten minutes. One minute of sex and nine minutes of guilt."

Karpinsky went to Rabbi Roth for advice. "Rabbi," he said, "I'm ruined. I'm a salesman, a respectable married man, but my life is ruined."

"What happened?" asked the rabbi.

"I was in Mobile, Alabama, coming home from dinner in a restaurant, and this big black man dragged me by the neck, and said to me, "You're gonna suck me off, you mocky son-of-a-bitch, or I'm gonna bust your head!' Rabbi, I'm ruined!"

"No, no," said the rabbi. "The Talmud rules that a man can do anything but spit on the Bible to save his life."

"Nooooh, Rabbi, I'm ruined," moaned Karpinsky. "I liked it!"

One day a Protestant minister came into Bonatelli's barbershop and got a haircut. When Bonatelli was finished, the minister reached for his wallet but the barber shook his head and smiled.

"Put-a your wallet away, Reverend," said the Italian. "I never charge a man of the cloth."

The minister thanked him and left, but he soon returned and presented the pious barber with a Bible.

A few hours later, Father Rourke entered the Italian's shop and he, too, got a haircut. Once again the barber refused to accept any payment.

"Forget it, Father," he said. "I no take-a money from a priest."

Father Rourke left shortly thereafter and returned with a crucifix, which he presented to Bonatelli as a token of his appreciation.

Toward evening a rabbi entered the shop. He also got a haircut. When the rabbi reached into his pocket, the barber waved the money aside.

"That's okay, Rabbi," said Bonatelli. "I no accept-a pay from men who do-a da Lord's work."

So the Rabbi left, and came back with another Rabbi!

Lightning flashed across the sky. Thunder rumbled. The rain fell in torrents.

Inside a little Bronx apartment, old Zelig awaited the end. At his bedside, his wife wept silently.

"I'm dying," said the elderly man. "Send for a priest."

"Send for a what?" exclaimed his shocked wife.

"A priest."

"Zelig," she cried, "you mean a rabbi!"

"No, no," said the old man, "a rabbi should go out on a night like this?"

How do you know Jesus Christ was Jewish?
He went into his father's business.

Mrs. Rosenbaum became stranded one evening in a very "exclusive" resort section of Cape Cod. "Exclusive" meant that Jews were excluded. She entered the town hotel and said to the desk clerk, "I would like a room."

"Sorry," he replied. "The hotel is full."

"Then why does the sign say ROOMS AVAILABLE?"

"We don't admit Jews."

"It so happens I converted to a Catholicism. Ask me any question and I'll prove it!"

"All right," said the desk clerk. "How was Jesus born?"

"By virgin birth. The mama's name was Mary and the papa's name was the Holy Spirit."

"Okay, where was Jesus born?"

"In a stable."

"That's right. And why was he born in a stable?"

"Because," Mrs. Rosenbaum snapped, "bastards like you wouldn't rent a room for the night to a Jewish woman!"

The young Rabbi finally decided that he must talk to the richest member of his congregation, no matter how much it hurt.

"Why," asked the Rabbi, "must you fall asleep when I'm preaching?"

"Let me explain something," answered the millionaire. "Would I fall asleep if I didn't trust you?"

Who is the chief Rabbi of the Eskimos?
Eskimoses.

Rabbi Glucksman was seated next to a Baptist minister on a flight to New York. The stewardess approached them and said, "May I serve you a cocktail?"

"I'll take a whiskey sour," said the Rabbi.

"And you, Reverend?" asked the hostess.

"Young lady," said the clergyman, "before I let liquor touch my lips I'd just as soon commit adultery."

"Miss," said Rabbi Glucksman, "as long as there's a choice, I'll have what he's having."

The Pilgrims settled in Jamestown. How did the Jews settle?

Twenty cents on the dollar.

Goldfarb was invited to a birthday party for the parish priest. Wanting to show his desire to be a good member of the community, he went to a jewelry store to get the good father a birthday present.

"What would you recommend?" asked Goldfarb of the store clerk.

"How about this lovely crucifix with Christ on it?"

"Do you think he'd like that?"

"Absolutely."

"How much is it?"

"One hundred and fifty dollars."

"One hundred and fifty dollars!" exclaimed Goldfarb. "Have you got one without the acrobat on it?"

Wrench: A Jewish resort with horses

A Jewish boy converted to Catholicism and eventually became a priest. He was finally reconciled with his heartbroken mother, who now introduces him to friends as "My son, the father."

It was a highway accident involving several cars. A few minutes after the crash, an elderly woman walked over to a man lying on the side of the road. "Mister, have the police come yet?" she asked.

"No," replied the victim.

"Has an ambulance been here yet?"

"No," breathed the man.

"Has the insurance company been here yet?"

"No."

"Listen," said the old lady, "do you mind if I lie down next to you?"

What is a psychiatrist?

A Jewish doctor who couldn't stand the sight of blood.

The Goldberg's son Jake refused to take school seriously. He never did homework and was constantly playing hookey.

The principal suggested they send him to a Yeshiva. The Goldbergs did, but after a few weeks he was expelled.

The Goldbergs knew that Catholic parochial schools were very strict, so they decided to send Jake to one. They enrolled him in Christ-the-King School for Boys, and warned their son to behave and to do his lessons, because this was his last chance. If he was thrown out now, he would be sent to a school for delinquents.

After a week of parochial school, Jake came home with terrific grades. Miraculously, he had been converted into a well-behaved, serious student.

"How come you changed all of a sudden?" asked Goldberg.

"Well," he answered, "when I saw a man hanging on a cross in every room, I figured I'd better not be a wise guy anymore."

This is a computer age. Pretty soon, there will be no more names, just numbers.

"Hello, I'm number 7463538839933694377."

"Funny, you don't look Jewish."

"I know. I had my number bobbed."

Greenberg, shabbily dressed and carrying two paper bags, was stopped by a customs inspector. "What have you got in the bags?" the official asked.

"I got twenty-five thousand dollars here, which I am bringing to Israel to donate."

"C'mon," sneered the official, "you don't look like

you got the price of a meal, how could you be donating twenty-five thousand dollars to the state of Israel?"

"Well, you see, I had a job in a men's room, and when the men came in I said to them, 'give to help Israel or I'll cut off your balls.'"

"All right, so you got twenty-five thousand dollars in one bag, but what's in the other bag?"

"Some men didn't want to donate."

The Russian Intelligence Agency intercepted a message that showed that Israel had just made an important atomic discovery. Anxious to find out what the Israelis were up to, they sent a Russian agent to Tel Aviv.

The spy was told to contact a man named Silverman. The password was "Volga boatman."

The agent flew to Tel Aviv and went to look up the contact. When he arrived at the apartment house, he found that three different Silvermans were listed as living there.

He decided to try one at a time, hoping to get the right one the first time. The agent knocked on the door at the first floor. "Yes?" said the man.

"Is your name Silverman?" asked the agent.

"Why, yes," replied the Israeli.

"Volga boatman," said the Russian.

"Oh," grinned the man. "You want Silverman the spy. He lives two flights up."

Who is the Jewish husband's dream woman?
    His mother.

The Jewish people are the greatest optimists on the face of the earth. They cut off a piece before they know how long it's going to grow!

What's the definition of a child prodigy?
    A B-student with Jewish parents.

161

Frilly Dilly: A Jewish fag who was circumcised with
pinking shears

During the reign of the Gestapo in Germany, Schloss
and Hirsch were walking along a Munich street, when
an SS officer approached them. Schloss had proper
credentials, but Hirsch did not.

"Quick," said Hirsch, "you run that way. The Nazi
will follow you and I'll be able to get away."

Schloss tore off in the direction indicated, pursued
by the SS man, while Hirsch escaped. When the Nazi
finally caught up, he demanded to see Schloss' papers.
He saw that they were in order.

"So why did you run?" he asked.

"I just took a physic," said Schloss, "and my
doctor told me to run after taking the medicine."

"But didn't you see me running after you?"

"Yeah, I thought maybe we both had the same
doctor, and you took a physic, too."

Did you hear about the new discotheque that just
opened in Tel Aviv?

It's called Let My People Go-Go.

A little old, bearded Jew accidentally brushed by a Nazi
officer and knocked him off balance. "Schwein!" roared
the German, clicking his heels.

"Solomon!" said the Jew, bowing politely. "Pleased
to meet you!"

Schneider was cornered by two rough Nazi black-
guards. They stood him up against a wall and interro-
gated him, "All right, Jew, tell us who was responsible
for the defeat of Germany in 1917?"

Schneider said, "The Jews and the bicycle riders."

One of the befuddled SS men asked, "Why the
bicycle riders?"

"Ah," answered their victim, "why the Jews?"

Wasserman and Rosenberg agreed to assassinate
Hitler. Through investigation they discovered that the
dictator passed a certain corner every day at twelve
noon.

The two men set up vigil at the appointed corner
and stood ready to rid the world of its biggest ogre.

At exactly twelve, the men grasped their guns in
anticipation. Five minutes went by and the Nazi leader
did not appear. At ten minutes past twelve Hitler still
did not come. Fifteen minutes later, there was still no
sign of him.

"My goodness," exclaimed Wasserman, "I hope
nothing's happened to the poor man!"

New Yorker Garfinkel had dinner every night at a
Second Avenue restaurant. One night he said to the
owner, "The food is good, but why are you so stingy
with the bread? Every night, only two slices of bread."

The next night, Garfinkel was served three slices
of bread with his dinner. But on the way out, the
counterman heard him mutter: "Only three slices. Ha!"

The next night, four slices appeared on Garfinkel's
table, and the night after, five. Still, he was not
satisfied. On the sixth night, as Garfinkel walked in,
the proprietor whispered to the waiter: "Take a long
loaf of French bread, cut it in two, and shut him up
once and for all."

Garfinkel sat down and the waiter brought the split
French loaf.

"Aha," said Garfinkel. "I see you're back to two
slices."

Kaminsky was telephoned by his bank that he had
overdrawn $12.40.

"Look up a month ago," said Kaminsky, "and see
how I stood."

After holding the phone a moment, the bank teller
reported, "You had a balance of two hundred five
dollars and fifteen cents!"

"Did I call you up?" asked Kaminsky.

Halperin and Jaffe were walking through Central Park on a freezing February day with their hands in their pockets.

"Hey," said Halperin, "why don't you say something?"

"Ah!" replied Jaffe, "freeze your own hands."

"Don't you think Horowitz is a good talker?"

"Bah! Mintz can out-argue him with one hand tied behind his back!"

What is the name of the first Jewish astronaut?

Nose Cohen.

Selma and Debbie, two girls from Brooklyn, traveled all the way up to the Bronx Zoo one day. They paused in front of first cage.

"What's them?" asked Selma.

"Them's monkeys," replied Debbie.

"How do you like that!" said the first Jewish girl. "From all those calluses on their asses, I thought they were Canasta players."

JEWISH NYMPHOMANIAC

A WOMAN WHO WILL ALLOW HER HUSBAND TO
MAKE LOVE TO HER AFTER SHE COMES HOME
FROM THE BEAUTY PARLOR

What does a Jewish wife do to keep her hands nice and soft?

Nothing.

In what month do Jewish women talk the least?
February.

Why does a Jewish wife close her eyes when having sex?
Heaven forbid she should see her husband having a good time.

If you want to see a couple who have lived together in perfect happiness for a decade, just look for a Jewish mother and her ten-year-old son.

It was a fearful night. Lightning shot through the sky and the thunder roared in blasts that would frighten a lion. The rain came down in sheets.

The door of Goodman's Bakery opened and Harvey, thoroughly drenched, came up to the counter and said, "Let me have two bagels."

"What," said Goodman, "you came out on a night like this just for two bagels?"

"Yes, that's all," answered Harvey. "Just one for me and one for Pauline."

"Who's Pauline?" asked the baker.

"Pauline is my wife," answered the man. "Would my mother send me out on a night like this?"

Why do Jewish women wear two-piece bathing suits?
To separate the milk from the meat.

Gomez picked up the gambling money in Mexico for the mob each week and delivered it to a California contact. One week it was discovered that one hundred and fifty thousand dollars was missing. Figglio, a hit man, was dispatched to Tijuana to find out what happened to the cash. Silverstein, a CPA who spoke Spanish, was sent along to act as interpreter.

The two men held Gomez at gun point in a tiny hotel room. "Ask him where the hundred and fifty grand is," sneered Figglio.

Gomez answered through Silverstein, "I don't know what you're talking about."

The hit man shot off Gomez' left ear. "Now explain to him I want the right answer or he loses the other ear."

"I don't know nothing!" said Gomez through the interpreter.

Figglio shot off the Mexican's right ear. "Tell him if he don't tell us where the loot is I'm gonna shoot off his balls one at a time."

"Okay," said Gomez in Spanish, "the money is in a suitcase in the trunk of my car."

Silverstein interpreted for the hit man, "He says he'd rather die than tell you where he's hidden the money."

MEXICAN

WHY did the Mexicans fight so hard to capture the Alamo?

So they would have four clean walls to write on.

What are the three most important Mexican holidays?
1. Cinco De Mayo.
2. Navidad.
3. October 11.
What's October 11?
That's when the new Chevvys come out.

Why don't Mexicans have barbecues?
How can you keep beans on a grill?

A group of tourists were being shown through the Grand Canyon. They came to the edge of a formation, looked down, and discovered something at the bottom of the canyon.

The guide put his field glasses to his eyes, focused, and discovered that there was a burro lying on its back dead with its feet up in the air.

Upon closer inspection, he saw a man pinned underneath the donkey obviously dead. The man was wearing a T-shirt that read: EVEL GONZALES.

Why can't a Mexican open a checking account in California?

He can't write his name small enough on a check with a spray can.

What do they call a Mexican who drives a Rolls Royce?
    A car thief.

Pedro: Father, I think I have committed big sin.
Priest: Why Pedro?
Pedro: I think I married my sister.
Priest: No, no Pedro. I've known you and Carlotta all your lives and you are not related. What in the world ever gave you the idea you married your sister?
Pedro: Last night we undress for bed, she look at me and say, "Oh, brother!"

"The sting of a big Mexican hornet can drive people insane."

"Yeah, but that's nothing compared with a little Spanish fly!"

Did you hear about the little Mexican boy who was told to write out the first stanza of the "Star Spangled Banner?" He began, "Jose, can you see?"

Manuel Garcia Lopez had a small farm on the outskirts of Guadalajara. He planted beans. The next day a tornado blew away the crop. Lopez went right to work and replanted. Two days later, a flood washed away all the seeds. Manuel planted once again. This time locusts ate up his entire crop.

Manuel Garcia Lopez knelt before the crucifix in the mission church and prayed. "Oh, Lord," he moaned. "I am a good Catholic. I give to charity. I go to church every Sunday. Why, why do these things happen to me?"

A voice thundered back, "Because I hate Mexicans."

What is long, brown, and has a cumulative I.Q. of eighty?

A Cinco de Mayo parade.

Feel Up: What you get at a Mexican service station

Comedian Jackie Kahane returned from a Mexican vacation and reported "the cost of living is still comparatively low. You can get five pounds of sugar, ten pounds of flour, a fifth of whiskey and a wife for ten dollars. Of course, it's cheap whiskey."

An airplane crossing the Atlantic ran into engine trouble. After dumping all the baggage to lighten the load, the pilot informed the passengers that three people would have to jump in order to save the rest.

"We need three volunteers!" announced the pilot.

Immediately, an Englishman left his seat, shouted "God Save the Queen," and jumped out.

In a little while, a Frenchman got up, said *"Vive la France,"* and took the plunge.

Five minutes later, a husky Texan from San Antonio stood up, screamed, "Remember the Alamo!" and threw a Mexican out the door.

There was a Senora from Alicante
Whose morals were notably scanty
  "I'm not at my best,"
  She said, "Overdressed."
So she left off both brassiere and panty.

Wet Back: Rio Grande surfer

A tourist got off the train in Mexico and noticed Salinas lying peacefully in the sun on the station platform. "Hey," he called, "why don't you get yourself a job?"

"Why?" said Salinas pleasantly.

"Well, wouldn't you like to have some money in the bank?"

Again the Mexican asked, "Why?"

"So you can retire," explained the tourist, annoyed, "and never work again!"

Salinas shrugged, "But I'm not working now!"

Did you hear about the Mexican who could only get up in the early morning?

He was known as Dawn Juan.

Zamora was riding a little mule and his wife was walking behind him.

"Friend, why is your wife not riding?" inquired a visitor.

The Mexican replied, "She ain't got no mule."

Senor Eeta: A Mexican pansy

At the International Gay Lib convention, two Spaniards prissied up to a Mexican. One Spanish fellow said, "Hi there, señor. This is my friend Juan, and I'm also Juan. I bet you are Juan, too!"

Martinez gazed through the bars at the county jailor.

"Can you read and write?" asked the jailor during the booking process.

"Can write, not read," replied the prisoner.

"Write your name then."

Martinez scrawled huge letters across the paper handed him. "What is that you wrote?" asked the jailor.

"I don't know," said the Mexican. "I told you I can't read."

Holston hired on as a ranch hand in Texas. One day he approached Davis, the foreman. "What do you do for fun out here on the prairie?"

"Well," replied the foreman, "we got a Mexican cook at the ranch, and every Saturday night we dress him in women's clothes and six of us take him dancing."

"Not me!" declared Holston, "I don't go for that kind of stuff."

"Neither does the Mex," said Davis. "That's why it takes six of us."

Titeria: A brassiere factory in Mexico

Fernando was getting married. There was a big wedding feast and the wine flowed like water. Things were going fine, until Fernando couldn't find his beautiful bride. After looking over the guests, he found his pal Luis was also missing.

Fernando started searching the premises. He looked into the bridal chamber and discovered Luis making love to his bride. Fernando closed the door softly, and crept down the stairs to his guests.

"Queek, queek! Everybody, come look," he shouted. "Luis ees so drunk, he theenk he ees me!"

Teacher: No, Manuela, second wind is not something a Mexican gets by eating refried beans.

Sanchez went up to his neighbor and asked:

"Pancho, do you like a woman who has a big stomach sticking all the way out?"

"No."

"Do you like a woman whose breasts hang almost to her knees?"

"No, señor, no."

"Would you like a woman whose backside is so *mucho grande*?"

"Caramba! No!"

"Then tell me, why do you keep screwing my wife?"

SIGN IN A SOUTH OF THE BORDER NIGHTCLUB
TRY OUR FRIJOLES AND YOU MIGHT
WIND UP WITH A HOT TAMALE

Irate bullfighter's wife to her triumphant toreador:

"Sure you were awarded the bull's ears, his tail, and his hooves, but the one thing of his you *could* have used you didn't get!"

A Texas cowboy was walking down a Tijuana street. Suddenly, young Pablo walked up to him and yanked on his sleeve.

"Hey, mister," said the boy, "you wanna make love to my seester?"

"Podnah," said the Texan, "ah don't even drink the water here!"

The local procurer in Mexico grabbed the distraught tourist stepping down the gangplank.

"I got a nice young girl for you, twelve years old, a virgin."

When the tourist refused, the procurer said, "Then I got a nice young boy for you, twelve years old, a virg—"

"Look!" roared the tourist, "I don't want a young girl, I don't want a young boy—I just want the American consul!"

"Hmmm," murmured the procurer, "very difficult—but I try."

Slappy White, the talented black comic, gets screams with this story:

"One time Redd Foxx and me went down to Tijuana in Mexico and we found this cute little monkey. Well, we wanted to bring it back to Los Angeles for a pet but we were afraid the customs inspectors wouldn't let us.

"So we went into this ladies' shop down on the main drag, bought the monkey a little dress and a hat, put it between us in the car and drove right up to the border gate.

"The Inspector looked in the car, asked if we had anything to declare, we said 'No,' so he waved us on.

"As we were pulling away, I heard one customs officer say to the other one, 'Ain't that the way it always happens! Any time you see a Mexican gal who looks halfway decent, she's out with a couple of spooks!"

The idea of daylight saving came from an old Mexican who cut off one end of his blanket and sewed it on the other end to make it longer.

Driscoll, a New Yorker, was visiting Mexico City when he spotted a pretty prostitute. He walked up to her and said, *"Soixante neuf? Sexaginta novem? Sesanta nueva?"*

"Talk Eengleesh," said the girl. "I can't count!"

La Cunta Junta: What the Women's Liberation Movement is called in Mexico.

Maxwell went to Acapulco during summer vacation. He didn't speak Spanish, so was at a loss when a voluptuous Latin beauty sat down next to him in a cantina.

After a while he asked hopefully, "Can you speak English?"

"Si, bot joos a leetle bit," she replied, flashing a warm smile.

"Just a little bit, huh?" the American repeated. "How much?"

"Twenty-five dollars," the senorita replied.

Raul was sitting against the wall of his friend Pablo's adobe shack. Pablo came out of the house with a butterfly in his hand.

"Ay, Pablo," called Raul. "Where are you going with the butterfly?"

"I'm going to get some butter," replied Pablo.

"Oh, you foolish fellow," said Raul. "You cannot get butter with a butterfly."

A few minutes later, to Raul's astonishment, Pablo returned with a bucket of butter.

In a little while, Pablo came out—this time carrying a jar of horseflies.

"Ay, Pablo," called Raul. "Where you going with them 'orseflies?"

"Where you think?" answered Pablo. "To get horses, of course."

Pablo returned in a few minutes, leading a pair of beautiful stallions.

"See! I tol' you," said Pablo to the amazed Raul.

Ten minutes later Pablo came out clutching a handful of pussy willows.

"Ay, Pablo!" shouted Raul, "Wait for me—I go with you!"

POLISH

How does a Polish airplane pilot navigate?
  By reading street signs.

Binkowski was stopped by his friend. "Why you look so
downhearted?"
  "I can't understand it," said the Polack. "My
neighbor took out fifty-thousand dollars worth of life
insurance and died anyway."

Zajackowski walked up to an airport ticket counter and
said, "When is the next plane to Buffalo?"
  "At five-thirty this afternoon," replied the clerk.
"But it's a local flight with stopovers in Washington
and New York. The whole flight will take about four
hours."
  "That be too long," said Zajackowski.
  "The best I can do is a direct flight the day after
tomorrow," said the clerk.
  "Okay, I wait for that one," said the Polack.

Piotr: Why does the Weather Bureau name hurricanes after girls?

Gregorz: I give up.

Piotr: If they name after boys, they would be called himicanes.

Bozniack became a successful businessman and was invited to give a speech at graduation of his former high school.

"Boys," he said, "always remember that education is a fine thing. Nothing like it. Take arithmetic, for example. Through education we learn that two twos are four, that four fours are eight, that eight eights — and then there's geography."

What do a football player and a Polish girl have in common?

They both shower after the fourth period.

Polish National Bank: Pole vault

"Did you see in the paper where this woman had a wooden baby?"

"How'd that happen?"

"She was screwed by a Pole."

A Polish couple decided to have a chicken farm. They bought two chickens, took them home, dug a hole in their back yard and buried the chickens head first. Next morning they discovered that the chickens were dead.

They bought two more chickens, this time planting them in the yard feet down. By the next morning, the fowl had died.

They wrote to the Polish counsel explaining their problem. Within a week they received a prompt reply from the Polish consul. The letter said, "Please send us a soil sample."

What's green and sits on the toilet?
A Polish girl scout doing her good deed for the
week.

A Madison Avenue advertising agency conducted a
survey in Europe to find out which was the most
popular feminine hygiene spray. These were the results:
In France it was Feminique.
In England it was Pristine.
And in Poland it was Janitor in a Drum.

"How be your wife?" asked Zimbriski.
"She's up in bed with laryngitis," replied
Raczkiewicz.
"Oh," said the other Polack, "is that Greek bastard
around again!"

Polish Lipstick: Preparation H

Puszko ordered lasagna for dinner in an Italian
restaurant. "Okay," said the waiter, "do you prefer red
or white wine?"
"It make no difference," said the Polack. "I be
color blind!"

What do they call a Polish prostitute?
A ski jump.

"Damn it!" exclaimed Bernacki. He was standing in a
bus, holding onto the strap with one hand while in his
other he clutched a heavy load of six-packs of beer.
"Can I help you?" asked another passenger.
"Yeah," answered the Polack. "Would you hold
onto this strap for me so I can get my fare out?"

Jan: I keep seeing spots before my eyes.
Piotr: Have you seen a doctor?
Jan: No, just spots.

Miss Luzinski was driving along the highway when a police car stopped her. The cop said, "Why don't you have a red light on this car?"

"It ain't that kind of car!" she retorted.

Mrs. Jablonski met a diplomat at a UN cocktail party. "What 'nese are you," she asked, "Japanese, Chinese, or Javanese?"

"I happen to be Japanese, madam," he said in impeccable English. "What kee are you? Monkee, donkee, or yankee?"

Disgusted with his players during practice, Coach Custak called them together and shouted, "Look, I'm convinced that before we can make any further progress we gotta go back to the fundamentals." He reached over and picked up a ball.

"Now this," he said, "is a football. It—"

Trablinski the tackle interrupted. "Please, coach, not so fast!"

What's green, purple, orange, chartreuse, pink, and red?

A Polish housewife going to church on Sunday.

How many Polacks does it take to paint a house?

1,001—one to hold the brush and 1,000 to move the house up and down.

Why don't they have any ice cubes in Poland?

The inventor died and took the recipe with him.

What do the numbers 1776 and 1492 have in common?
They are adjoining rooms at the Warsaw Hilton.

Lotacki was looking around the sidewalk on his hands and knees in front of his neighbor's house.
"You lose something?" asked his neighbor.
"Yeah," said the Polack. "My watch."
"Where exactly did you drop it?"
"In the cellar."
"Then why are you looking for it out here in the street?"
"Well, it be dark down in the cellar—there be more light out here under street lamp."

Polish Cocktail: A mushroom in a glass of beer

Carolyn, a curvaceous traveling saleslady, was waiting her turn to register at a motel when she overheard the desk clerk tell Zabrocki, the man in front of her, that he'd just gotten the last room. She waited for the Polack to leave the desk and then approached.
"There isn't another motel within miles and I'm dead tired," she pleaded. "Look—you don't know me, I don't know you, they don't know us, we don't know them. How's about me spending the night with you?"
"I don't care," said Zabrocki.
They went to his room; he took off his clothes and so did she.
"Listen," she said, "you don't know me, I don't know you, they don't know us, we don't know them. Let's have a few drinks. I got a bottle."
After they'd gotten a little high, she cuddled up to him and whispered, "You don't know me, I don't know you, they don't know us, we don't know them—let's have a party."
"Hey," said the Polack. "If I don't know you and you don't know me and they don't know us and we don't know them—who the hell we gonna invite?"

Did you hear about the Polish girl who lost her mind?
For ten years she worked in a house of ill repute.
Then she found out the rest of the girls got paid.

Kozlow: I caught my wife on the couch with 'nother
man last night. But I got even with him.
Halick: What'd you do?
Kozlow: I turned out the lights so he couldn't see what
he was doing.

"How'd you make out last night with that Polish
chick?"
"She was kind of leery about checking into the
Cadillac Hotel in Detroit. She thought it was only for
rich cars."

"Say, how come you got home so early from your date
last night?" Domanski was asked.
"Well," he replied, "after the show we go up to her
apartment. We listened to records, talked for a while,
had a couple drinks—and then she reached over and
turned out all the lights."
"Yes?" coaxed his roommate.
"So I can take a hint—I went home."

Sobczvk, the master of a Polish ship, was observed to
go to his safe, unlock it, extract a large black book,
read carefully, replace it in the safe, and lock it up.
The other officers on board were most curious but
could never get hold of the old man's keys.
One day, Sobczvk died and was buried at sea. The
chief officer found the keys, unlocked the safe and
anxiously opened the book. There was a single entry:
"Port is the left, starboard the right."

Wojcik asked for work in a Detroit railroad yard, said that he was willing to do anything.

"Okay," said the foreman. "Take this oil can and oil all the switch points and crossings up the line."

Two months later, the foreman received this telegram:

DEAR SIR: ARRIVED AT BALTIMORE. PLEASE FORWARD MORE OIL.

Who are the four most dangerous people in the world?
A Jew with an attorney.
A Greek with sneakers.
A Frenchman with a jagged tooth.
A Polack with a credit card.

What love song does a Polish boy sing to a Polish girl in a canoe on a moonlit lake?
"The Beer Barrel Polka."

Everyone knows Cortez discovered Mexico and that Columbus discovered America, but who discovered Poland?
The Roto Rooter man.

Why does a Polack eat beans for dinner on Saturday night?
So he can take a bubble bath Sunday morning.

A Cleveland streetwalker picked up Cusick in the park. She took him to her apartment, promptly undressed, and got into bed.

He, too, got out of his clothes but left his shoes on.

"Come now," she said, "we can't have that. Take off your shoes."

"What," said the Polack, "and maybe catch athlete's foot?"

Did you hear about the Polish hemophiliac who tried to cure himself with acupuncture?

Pulski was visiting New York. He met Swirta.
Swirta: Hullo, Pulski, when did you come over?
Pulski: Yesterday.
Swirta: How you come; by sea or air?
Pulski: I don't know. My wife buy the ticket.

Rodeck, walking down lower Broadway on a dark night, passed an alley. Two thugs jumped on him, and though he put up a terrific fight, they got him down.

After they searched him they were amazed at the small amount of money they found in his pockets. "You mean you put up that fight for sixty-seven cents?" they asked.

"Hell, no," answered the Polack. "I thought you be after the five hundred dollar in my shoe."

Sophie, the new maid, answered the phone. "Yes, you be right," she said, and hung up the receiver.

Again the phone rang and she answered, "Yes, ma'am, it sure is!" and hung up again.

"Who was that?" asked her employer.

"I don't know," replied the Polish girl. "Some crazy lady keep saying, 'It's a long distance from New York,' and I said, 'It sure is.'"

Did you hear about the two Polacks who hijacked a submarine and asked for a million dollars and two parachutes?

What does it say on the bottom of a Coke bottle manufactured in Poland?
    Open other end.

Klonsinski and Cieslak were working on a building site.

Suddenly, Klonsinski shouted, "Watch out, the bricks are falling out of the wall."

Just then, a brick fell and hit Cieslak, taking off his ear. He lay on the ground bleeding profusely.

"Take it easy," said Klonsinski, "I find your ear and take you to hospital. They soon sew it back on."

Klonsinski searched among the rubble, found Cieslak's ear, and took it over to where he was lying.

"O.K.," says Klonsinski. "I got it."

Cieslak looked at it and cried, "That not be mine, you dumbbell! Mine had a cigarette behind it."

Sobczuk, a newly arrived immigrant, walked up to a traffic cop. "Hey, Mr. Policeman," he said, "can you tell me right time?"

"Three o'clock," the patrolman replied.

"God damn!" said the Polack. "What going on in this country? Every time I ask somebody for time I get different answer."

Magda got a job in the Klein household shortly after her arrival in this country.

"Have you changed the water in the goldfish bowl like I told you?" asked Mrs. Klein.

"There be no need to," said the Polish girl. "They no drunk up water I put in there last month."

How do you explain a black man with a white penis?

Easy! A Polack coal miner who goes home for lunch.

Did you hear about the Polack who donated blood to the blood bank and complained because they didn't give him a toaster?

Mr. and Mrs. Brezliki were boarding the cruise ship for a long-awaited trip to the South Seas when Mr. Brezliki said, "Gee, Maggie, I wish I'd brought along the ice box."

"Are you crazy, honey?" said his wife irritably. "What makes you say a thing like that?"

"Because I left our two tickets on top of it."

Lomnicki lurched up to the airline counter and said to the clerk, "I want buy round-trip ticket, honeybunch."

"Of course, sir," said the clerk. "Where to?"

"Right back here," replied to Polack.

Zalewski got a job as a delivery boy in a pet shop. One day he was told to deliver a pet rabbit to Mrs. Caldwell, Route 2—Box 4.

"You better write that down in case I forget it," said the boy.

Slipping the address into his pocket, Zalewski started off on his errand. Every few minutes he glanced at the address and said, "I know where I'm going. Mrs. Caldwell, Route Two—Box Four."

Everything went smoothly until he hit a huge hole in the road. The truck landed in a ditch and the rabbit began to run for its life across an open field.

Zalewski stood there laughing uproariously. A passerby stopped and asked, "What's so funny?"

"Did you see that crazy rabbit running across that field?" said the Polack. "He doesn't know where he's going 'cause I've got the address in my pocket."

Did you hear about the Polish parachute?

It opens on impact.

Kozien invited his black friend Otis to his home in Buffalo for the weekend. They had been close buddies in high school. Otis had just been released from jail after two years, and arrived at Kozien's home as horny as a ram. During the first night, after a big dinner and a quart of bourbon, Otis screwed the Polack's mother, his wife, and two daughters before he finally passed out.

Next morning when he came down for breakfast, the angry Polack was waiting at the bottom of the stairs. "You go through my whole family like a buzz saw," shouted Kozien, "and for me you don't even have time for a goodnight kiss!"

Buczkowski stormed into a musical instrument store and began yelling at the manager.

"What seems to be the trouble, sir?" asked the manager.

"You be bunch of damn cheaters," yelled the Polack. "Last week I buy piano stool here and no matter how I twist and turn the lousy thing I no can get it to play one single note."

Mrs. Siwicki knitted a sweater for her husband, who was in the Army and stationed in Hawaii. When the Polish woman mailed it, she enclosed this note: "Air mail costs so much for each ounce that I have cut all the buttons off your sweater. P.S. You'll find them all in the right-hand pocket."

"Did you ever meet me before?" demanded Piwalski.

"No," confessed the stranger.

"Then how do you know it's me?"

Did you hear about the Polish girl who was a very considerate pianist?

She wears gloves when she plays so as not to wake the neighbors!

"All bankers must be Polish!"

"Why?"

"If bankers could count, why do they always have eight windows and two tellers?"

Wajda: How come you bought a baby turtle as a pet?
Pracki: They say turtles live for two hundred years and I wanted to see if it was true.

Did you hear about the Polack who wanted to get revenge on a restaurant he thought charged too much?

He went in, ordered the most expensive dinner on the menu, paid for it, and then sneaked out without eating it.

Filipowicz wanted a divorce from his wife.

"Why?" asked the Judge.

"Well," replied the Polack, "she be trying to kill me."

"How do you know that?" asked the magistrate.

"Yesterday, in the bathroom I find a bottle that say Polish Remover."

A Frenchman, a German, and a Pole wanted to see the track and field events at the Olympics but all the seats were sold out. They devised a way to get in.

The Frenchman walked up to the gate carrying a javelin. "Flambeau!" he announced to the gateman, "Javelin!" He was passed through.

The German arrived at the gate carrying a discus. "Rhinehart! Discus!" He was let in.

The Polack showed up with barbed wire wrapped around his shoulders. "Grabowski! Fencing!"

Did you hear about the two Polacks who went to a drive-in movie?

They didn't like the picture so they slashed their seats.

"Glowicki, you're working too hard carrying bricks up and down the ladder at that terrific speed."

"Be quiet. I fool them all. They be the same bricks all the time."

Polaski and Cusick were driving through the back roads of Maine when they came to one of the state's famous covered bridges. The sign at the top said: CLEARANCE TEN FEET.

Polaski and Cusick measured the height of their camper. "It be eleven feet," said Cusick.

"How high be the bridge?" asked Polaski.

"It say ten feet."

"Ah, come on, let's take a chance," said Cusick, "there be no cops around!"

What is the national drink of Poland?

Peanut Butter.

Irena had every curve in exactly the right place. The first day on the job the office manager approached her. "Do you like cocktails?" he asked.

"I don't know," said the Polish girl. "Why don't you tell me one."

Did you hear about the two Polacks who froze to death in a drive-in movie?

They went to see *Closed for the Winter*.

What happens when you cross a Jew with a Polack?

You get a janitor who owns the building.

Three sailors, a Frenchman (Gaston), a Swede (Swen), and a Pole (Rojak) were stationed on a lonely island in the Pacific. Without a woman for months, they sent away to a mail order company for a woman made of rubber. When it arrived they blew it up and Gaston spent the night with it.

In the morning, the Frenchman reported, "It was wonderful. Just like my woman back in Paris."

Swen's turn came that evening, and the next day he said, "Guys, that was the greatest sex I've had in my life."

As soon as it turned dark, Rojak disappeared with the rubber woman. In the morning his buddies asked how he liked it. "Not too good," said the Polack. "I bit her on the tit, she farted, and flew out the window."

How many Polacks does it take to make love?

Three—two to do it and one to read the instructions out of the book.

Why did the Polack stop at the house of ill-repute?

He was waiting for the light to change.

What happened when they dropped the atom bomb on Warsaw?

It did $10.15 worth of damage.

"Pa, I wanna go to college," said Leon.

"Do you know what's what?"

"Huh?"

"Do you know 'what's what'? Go into the bathroom and think for a few minutes and if you find out 'what's what,' I send you to college."

Leon went into the bathroom, thought a few minutes, came out and said, "Pa, I don't know 'what's what.'"

"Sure you don't know 'what's what.' Go and get yourself a job and when you find out 'what's what' I send you to college."

Leon left, went to a nearby bar, and began drinking. He met Alice, a blond sitting at the bar. Soon, they wound up at her apartment. After a few drinks she said, "Excuse me while I slip into something more comfortable."

Alice returned a few moments later, completely nude.

Leon looked at her and said, "What's this?"

"What's what?" she asked.

"If I knew what's what, I'd be in college!"

The college professor told his creative writing class to prepare a short story embodying all of the following elements: religion, sex, mystery, royalty.

Jachienicz turned in this sentence:

"'Good God,'" said the Polish homecoming queen, "'I'm pregnant. Who did it?'"

Did you hear about the Polack who spent a fortune to build a storm cellar in case of an earthquake?

Several years ago in New York, it was proposed that a gondola should be put in the Central Park lake. The Polish councilman supported the idea with enthusiasm.

"Let's get two gondolas. Male and female."

There is a box of candy on a table. Beside it are Santa Claus, the Easter Bunny, a dumb Italian, and a smart Polack. Who gets the candy?

The dumb Italian—because the others are charitable and there's no such thing as a smart Polack.

Mrs. Callin was showing a contractor through the second floor of her new house to advise him what colors to paint the rooms.

"I'd like the bathroom done in white!"

The contractor walked over to the window and shouted: "Green up! Green up!"

"I want the bedroom in blue!" continued the woman.

The contractor yelled out the window, "Green up! Green up!"

"The halls should be done in beige!"

Again the man barked out the window, "Green up! Green up!"

"Will you stop that?" ordered Mrs. Callin. "Everytime I give you a color I want, you shout 'Green up!' What in God's name does that mean?"

"I'm terribly sorry, Madam!" explained the contractor. "But I've got three Polacks down there putting in the lawn!"

Wiznicki and Polacek went to a used car lot to buy a car. They didn't have enough money to buy one but the salesman sold them a camel.

"Does this thing work?" asked Wiznicki.

"Of course," said the salesman. "This camel stops at red lights and goes on green."

Wiznicki and Polacek left on the back of the camel but in twenty minutes they were back without the animal.

"What happened?" asked the salesman.

"Camel do what you say all right," exclaimed Polacek. "We stop at red light, boys in car pull up beside us. One boy yell out, 'Look at those two jerks on the camel.' We got off to see who the two jerks were and camel ran away!"

Pieracki, a Pole, Odum, a Black, and Alvarez, a
Mexican, were out of work and living together. Pieracki
came home one night and announced he had gotten a
job. "Hey, fellas, wake me up tomorrow at six," he
said, "I have to be at work by six-thirty!"

While Pieracki slept, Odum said to Alvarez, "He
got a job because he's white. We can't get one because
I'm black and you're brown." So during the night they
put shoe black all over Pieracki. Then they agreed to
wake him late.

Next morning when Pieracki arrived at work, the
foreman said, "Who are you?"

"You hired me yesterday," he replied. "You told me
to be here at six-thirty!"

"I hired a white man—you're black!"

"I am not!"

"Yes you are! Go look in the mirror!"

The Polack rushed over to a mirror, looked at
himself and exclaimed, "My God! They woke up the
wrong one!"

How does a Polish mother put on her child's
underwear?
Yellow in front, brown in back.

Why are Polish mothers so strong and square-
shouldered?
From raising dumbbells.

Marlene and Florence, two Denver secretaries, were
chatting over lunch. "I was raped last night by a
Polack," whispered Marlene.

"Really?" said Florence. "How did you know he
was Polish?"

"I had to help him."

191

Did you hear about the Polish couple who had a double ring ceremony?

They were married in a bathtub.

POLISH WEDDING GOOD LUCK GUIDE FOR THE BRIDE

SOMETHING OLD,

SOMETHING NEW,

SOMETHING BORROWED,

SOMETHING BLUE,

SOMETHING RED,

SOMETHING ORANGE,

SOMETHING PURPLE,

SOMETHING . . .

How can you tell the groom at a Polish wedding?
   (a) He's the one with the dirty T-shirt.
   (b) He's the one with the white bowling shoes.
   (c) He's the one not wearing the bowling shirt.
   (d) He's the one wearing the tuxedo and combat
       boots.

How can you tell the bride at a Polish wedding?

She's the one with the braided armpits and sequins on her sneakers.

How can you tell a mother-in-law at a Polish wedding?

She's the one on her hands and knees picking up the rice.

Why did the bride think she had the poshest Polish wedding in Poland?

Her veil practically covered her overalls.

When Zelda returned from her honeymoon, she telephoned the doctor. "Those birth control pills you gave me aren't working."

"What do you mean, not working?" asked the surprised physician. "I just gave them to you a week ago!"

"I know," said the Polish girl, "but they keep falling out!"

What do they call a stork that delivers Polish babies? A dope peddler.

One of the first campaign promises the recently elected mayor of New York made was to clean up the city. He declared war on the rats. His Honor ordered the health inspector to send nine Polish exterminators down into the sewers to wipe out the rodents.

A month later, only six of the nine Poles came back. "All right," demanded the Mayor, "what happened to the other three men?"

"They defected to the enemy," explained the inspector. "And out of the six that returned, two brought back war brides."

PUERTO RICAN

Why don't Puerto Rican girls shave their legs?
They think textured stockings are still in.

Why do Puerto Ricans need such fat wallets?
To carry all their food stamps.

What is the name of the world-renowned Puerto Rican
expert on baby care?
Dr. Spick.

What does 1-C represent?
The apartment number of a Puerto Rican
penthouse.

What do you get when you cross a Puerto Rican with an Italian?
Bad breath.

"Whenever I'm in the dumps, I buy me a new dress," Rosalie confided to her friend.
"I was wondering where you got those things," muttered the friend.

Where did the limbo originate?
In a Greyhound bus terminal. A Puerto Rican was trying to get into a pay toilet.

What do they call a Puerto Rican girl who is pretty?
Italian.

What does a Puerto Rican have in the front of his pants?
A Spanish fly.

What is the Puerto Rican national anthem?
"We'll take Manhattan, the Bronx, and Staten Island too. . . ."

NEWS ITEM

FORTY-FIVE PUERTO RICANS WERE
ARRESTED FOR SLEEPING IN CENTRAL PARK.
THEY PLEADED NOT GUILTY. THEIR
DEFENSE WAS THAT THEY WERE HAVING
THEIR ROOM PAINTED.

"I can't go out with you tonight," said Maria.
"Why not?" asked Arturo.
"My little sister is getting married and I'm the only one there is to stay home with her baby."

Why did the Puerto Rican have scratches all over his face?
     From learning to eat with a knife and fork.

What's a Puerto Rican limousine?
     A garbage truck with Mercedes hubcaps.

What's a Puerto Rican safari?
     Three roaches and a can of Raid.

Where do you find the best Puerto Rican drama?
     Night court.

Did you hear about the Puerto Rican secretary who is getting so experienced, she can type twenty mistakes a minute?

Why aren't Puerto Ricans allowed to swim in the Hudson?
     They leave a ring around the river.

Carmencita was a very good worker, but she was fired from her job at the sanitary napkin factory. They found her putting get-well cards in each carton.

How can you tell the difference between a Puerto Rican and a gorilla?
     The gorilla peels the banana before he eats it.

What did the Puerto Ricans decide to do about the gas shortage?
     Eat more beans.

What's the difference between a Puerto Rican and a peanut butter sandwich?

A Puerto Rican doesn't stick to the roof of your mouth.

Rico walked into the bar sporting a big black eye. "Hey man, what happened to you?" asked one of the guys.

"I called my chick a two-bit whore," Rico replied.

"Man! What did she hit you with?" the guy asked.

Rico shrugged. "A bag of quarters."

Hubcap: Puerto Rican pizza popper

Where is the greatest supply of gold in Puerto Rico located?

On the two upper front teeth.

What have Puerto Ricans contributed to the air pollution problem?

About 90 percent.

What do they do with the garbage from Italian restaurants?

They serve it for dinner in Puerto Rican restaurants.

Did you hear about the town in New Jersey that's so poor that the head of the Mafia is Puerto Rican?

Since Carmelita raised her price to three dollars, she's known in Spanish Harlem as the high-priced spread.

Why does a Puerto Rican on a suspension bridge
represent cleanliness?
Because it's spic and span.

What's a Puerto Rican butler?
A trained cockroach on a leash.

What is the official Puerto Rican mascot?
The litterbug.

"I heard you just bought a rifle."
"Yeah. I'm gonna shoot me some cans."
"Cans?"
"Uh-huh! Africans, Mexicans, and Puerto Ricans."

What did the Chinaman say when he saw his first
crowd of Puerto Ricans?
"I can't tell them apart."

Alzado was an honest, hard-working man. One day he
went into a neighborhood grocery store. Instead of
offering to pay with food stamps or a phony credit card,
he put cash on the counter.
The clerk said, "Do you have any I.D., sir?"

Why don't Puerto Ricans watch "Hee-Haw"?
Because they can't find "Jee-Jaw" listed anywhere
in the *TV Guide*.

How did the Puerto Rican improve his social standing?
He ran off with gypsies.

Did you hear about the Puerto Rican surgeon who made medical history recently?

He performed the first appendix transplant on record.

What do you get when you cross a Puerto Rican with a gorilla?

A monkey with sideburns.

A Communist demagogue was on a soapbox in lower Manhattan, making the usual pitch about the glorious new world that would arise under the new order of things. "Each man will be a king," he proclaimed. "We will eat strawberries and cream and no man will be required to perform any menial, undignified tasks."

Then a heckler called out, "Who's gonna sweep the streets, then?"

"The Puerto Ricans," replied the Communist.

What's a Puerto Rican day in the country?

Playing in an empty lot.

Why do Puerto Ricans feed cockroaches?

They keep them as house pets.

Why are computer centers in Puerto Rico such a miserable failure?

Because the technician on night duty always forgets to stoke up the furnace.

Why did the Puerto Rican salute the box of Corn Flakes in the supermarket?

Because the label read General Foods.

SURE SIGN OF INFLATION
A VOLKSWAGEN CAREENING DOWN THE STREET
WITH ONLY NINE PUERTO RICANS IN IT

How does a hip black pimp get his customized Cadillac greased?

He just runs over the nearest Puerto Rican.

Fuentes and Ruiz met on the street one day.

"Hey, man" said Fuentes, "how's that chick of yours?"

"Not so good," replied Ruiz. "She bled to death."

"Bled to death!" repeated Fuentes. "From what?"

"Gonorrhea," Ruiz answered.

"Man, people don't bleed to death from gonorrhea," Fuentes argued.

"They do when they give it to me!" said Ruiz.

RUSSIAN

At an art exhibition in Moscow, one exhibit was a huge success—a painting of a loaf of bread and two sausages.

Everyone wanted to know the artist's name and address.

Migalovitch lay dying in his apartment when there was a loud knock on the door.

"Who is there?" called the dying man.

"The angel of death," a voice answered.

"Thank goodness," sighed the Russian. "I thought it was the secret police."

PARTY PROCLAMATION
AMERICAN COMUNISTS HEREAFTER
WILL NOT MEET IN GATHERINGS LARGER
THAN THREE PERSONS, THUS SHORTENING
THE ODDS ON WHICH ONE IS THE FBI
UNDERCOVER MAN.

A Soviet archaeological expedition in Egypt was given a mummy by Sadat, and they sent it back to Russia for study. They wanted to determine the mummy's age. But the scientists were pushed aside by the secret police who said, "Leave it to us; we'll find out."

Presently the secret police announced that the mummy's age was 4,840 years.

"Amazing," cried the Soviet scientists. "How did you determine it?"

"Easy," said the secret police. "The mummy confessed."

At a Russian factory, workers were asked to choose a new workers' committee by secret ballot.

Each man, upon approaching the ballot box, was handed a sealed envelope and told to deposit it through the slot at the top of a cardboard box.

Vasili slit open the envelope and began to examine the ballot. "Hey," shouted a supervisor. "You can't do that."

"But I want to know who I'm voting for," explained the worker.

"You must be mad," claimed the supervisor. "Don't you realize that the ballot is secret in the Soviet Union?"

Mrs. Zhvkov wanted to purchase a two-wheel bicycle for her son. The store had only tricycles.

"No, that is not what I want."

"You buy the tricycle," said the storekeeper. "After a week or so, one of the wheels will fall off."

Two strangers stopped to admire a handsome new automobile parked at a curb in Prague.

"Beautiful model!" enthused one. "Another great triumph for Soviet initiative and ingenuity!"

The other protested, "But that's an American car. Don't you know one when you see it?"

"Of course I do," snapped the first stranger. "But I don't know you!"

Mikoyan and Krushchev were discussing what to do with Stalin's body when it was removed from the Lenin mausoleum. "What about sending it to Israel?"

"Oh, no," said Krushchev, "I recall that a long time ago in Israel a man once rose from the dead."

"Who is your father?" a schoolboy was asked by Krushchev when he was in charge of Soviet Russia.

"Nikita Krushchev is my father," replied the lad.

"And who is your mother?"

"The Communist Party."

"Very good. Now tell me, what would you like to be when you grow up?"

"An orphan," replied the child.

When Stalin's body was removed from the Lenin mausoleum in Red Square and buried near the Kremlin walls, a small boy asked his grandmother, "What kind of a man was Lenin?"

"Lenin was a very great man," she said.

"And what kind of man was Stalin?" asked the child.

"Sometimes he was a very evil man," said the old woman.

"Babushka, what kind of a man is Leonid Brezhnev?"

"It is difficult to say, child," replied the grandmother. "When he dies, maybe we will find out."

An American and a Russian were engaging in the inevitable controversy concerning their respective concepts of democracy. "Any man in the land," said the American, "can go to Washington, ask to see the President, walk into his office and say, 'Mr. President, you stink!' and nothing will happen to him."

"And in Russia," said the Soviet defender, "any peasant can sneak away from his home, hitch a ride on a freight train, arrive in Moscow, show the secret police his identification card, walk into the Premier's office, sneak past the guards and say, 'Sir, the American President stinks,' and nothing will happen to him."

An American Communist arrived in Moscow to get fresh instructions from his Soviet masters. He approached a taxicab and asked, "Are you free?"

"Not me," snarled the Russian driver, "I'm a Russian."

The Russian Premier was inspecting a battalion of soldiers in Siberia. The men stood at attention with the temperature sixty below zero; snow up to their knees; frozen to their guns. The Premier walked down the line padded in twenty pounds of fur coat and two quarts of vodka. Suddenly he stopped, shoved his face at one of the men and asked "Comrade! How goes it?"

"I can't complain," said the soldier.

"You bet your life, you can't!"

A Soviet top-sergeant, instructing a bunch of new recruits, asked, "What does a good people's soldier do when he hears the command, 'Volunteers forward?'"

From the rear came a reply, "He steps back so as not to get in the way of the people's heroes!"

Kolchak was found fit for travel to the moon, but he told the commissar he didn't want to go space traveling.

"Where would you like to go?"

"To the United States."

"We can only take you to the moon," said the commissar. "If we could go to America, I'd go there myself."

A Russian lecturer was telling Czech students in Prague about the Soviet's wonderful scientific advances. "Already," he said, "we have launched two satellites. In no time at all we will be able to go to the moon. In a matter of a few years we will be able to go to Mars, and then to Venus. And later on to all the planets. Isn't this a wonderful thing?"

All the students nodded.

"Are there any questions?"

"Sir," a student asked, "when can we go to Vienna?"

"Why do we love the Soviet Union?" asked the teacher in Siberia.

"Because it has liberated us," replied the pupil.

"And why do we hate the United States?"

"Because it has not liberated us," was the reply.

Drag Nyet: Police raid on tranvestites

Popov left Moscow for Poland and sent back a postcard reading, "Greetings from free Warsaw." He traveled on to Czechoslovakia and sent a postcard reading, "Greetings from free Prague."

His next stop was Hungary, and from there Popov sent "Greetings from free Budapest." After a longer interval, a card from Vienna. It read, GREETINGS FROM FREE POPOV.

After waiting in line in front of a "people's store" for a long time, a Soviet citizen finally reached the counter and started to read from his shopping list. "Do you have any coats?" he began.

"Sorry," the clerk replied, "there aren't any."

"Then do you have any shirts?"

"We're out of shirts, too."

"Do you have any socks left? I need some very badly," asked the would-be customer.

"They're all gone, too," shouted the clerk, "and don't bother me any more. This is a store—not an information bureau!"

Two political prisoners in Budapest were trying to console one another before they went to trial. "If only I hadn't confessed," mourned one, "that I bought butter on the black market."

"That was a mistake," admitted the other. "Why did you confess that?"

"I had to!" he answered. "The man questioning me was the one who sold me the butter."

A factory worker in Budapest went up to the lady foreman and asked, "May I leave at the end of eleven and a half hours this evening instead of twelve, Madam Director? I'd like to go to the state opera."

"You may," decided the director. "I'm happy that our workers appreciate culture. But cut that 'Madam Director' business. Now that we have been liberated, remember we are all comrades! By the way, what opera are you seeing?

"*Comrade Butterfly.*"

Semyonov, a local party secretary, stopped Kagonovich on the street. "Comrade," he asked "why don't you come for ideological instruction every Tuesday and Thursday evening?"

"I don't need it," said Kagonovich.

"Who was Karl Marx?" asked Semyonov.

"I don't know."

"Who was Vladimir Lenin?"

"I don't know."

Semyonov went on and on. Finally Kagonovich interrupted, "You ask me who is this and who is that. Let me ask you! Who is Rudolph Ulyanov?"

"I don't know," said the secretary.

"Ah," said Kagonovich, "but I know that one. While you're at ideological instruction every Tuesday and Thursday night, Rudolph Ulyanov is screwing your wife!"

Kuropatkin and Davidov were scaling a treacherous mountain with the aid of some rope. Kuropatkin was obviously terrified. Davidov, noticing this, said, "You should not climb a mountain if you're afraid of it."

"It's not the mountain that worries me. It's the rope. I work in the factory that makes it."

A German in the Soviet Zone was accosted by a Communist Party member on a lonely road and relieved of all his possessions except his shirt.

"Could I have two marks back?" pleaded the German.

"Why?" asked the Communist.

"Well, sir," the German answered, "I haven't paid my dues to the Organization for German-Soviet Friendship and I don't want to lose my good standing."

At a Communist Party convention, one of the delegates kept yelling, "Long live Brezhnev!"

The chairman tried to hush him, saying, "Remember, you used to yell "Long live Khruschev.'"

"Right," said the delegate, "and is he living?"

American industrialization has finally penetrated Russia. In Moscow they have vending machines that sell diet borscht.

A German in the Soviet Zone reported to the police that his parrot was missing. He was asked whether the parrot talked. "Yes," he replied, "but any political opinions he expresses are strictly his own."

A candidate for the Communist Party was undergoing an oral examination. "What would you do, Comrade, if you were left two million rubles?"

"I would give one-half to the party and keep the other half for myself."

"Excellent! What would you do if you had two houses?"

"I would keep one and give the other to the state."

"Very wise. And what would you do if you had two pairs of shoes?"

The Comrade didn't answer.

"Comrade," said the Chairman, "you gave excellent answers to two difficult questions—and now you hesitate."

"Yes, Comrade Chairman. I haven't got a million rubles; I shall never have two houses; but I do have two pairs of shoes and I need them both!"

An Englishman, a Frenchman, and a Russian were trying to define true happiness.

"True happiness," said the Englishman, "is when you return home tired after work and find a gin and tonic waiting for you."

"You English have no romance," countered the Frenchman. "True happiness is when you go on a business trip, find a pretty girl who entertains you, and then you part without regrets."

"You are both wrong," concluded the Russian. "Real true happiness is when you are home in bed at four o'clock in the morning and there is a hammering at the front door and there stand members of the Secret Police, who say to you, 'Igor Zhvkovski, you are under arrest,' and you are able to reply, 'Sorry! Igor Zhvkovski lives next door!' "

"Why is Communism superior to other systems?" asked the Russian teacher.

"Because it copes successfully with difficulties that do not exist in other systems," replied the much-too-wise student.

The Russian rabbit fled across the border at Brest and didn't stop until a Polish rabbit assured him he was in Poland. "Why are you running?" asked the Polish rabbit.

"Because they're castrating all the camels in Russia," said the Russian bunny.

"But you're not a camel. You're a rabbit."

"Yes, but they castrate first and ask questions afterward."

Meeting in the park, a huge boxer stopped and wagged his tail in friendly greeting to a Russian wolfhound.

"How do you like America?" he asked.

"Well, it's different from my homeland," said the wolfhound. "In Russia I eat bones dipped in vodka and caviar. In Russia I have my own doghouse made of rare Siberian wood. In Russia, I sleep on a rug made of thick warm ermine."

"Then why did you come to America?"

"I like to bark once in a while."

An American visiting Leningrad was trying out his transistor radio while riding on a train. Menshikov sitting next to him watched with great curiosity.

"We have those, too," said the Russian. "What is it?"

At a disarmament conference in Geneva, an American delegate, stretching his legs under the table, accidentally bumped the knee of a Russian lady interpreter sitting directly across from him. He smiled an apology.

The lady neither spoke nor smiled. She turned to the Communist diplomat next to her and asked him something. The diplomat turned to his superior and whispered something to him. The chief then got up, left the table and went to the phone center. The meeting was recessed.

Two and one-half hours later it was resumed. The ranking diplomat returned to the table, spoke to his assistant, who whispered something to the lady interpreter, who looked across at the American delegate and said, "Your place or mine?"

A new jet plane transported Godunov from Pinsk to Minsk in four minutes and thirty-two seconds. He was overwhelmed. Godunov rushed to the home of Kolokov in Minsk and cried, "What a nation we have! Not only the greatest constitution, the greatest leaders, and the greatest army, but now we have a wonderful plane that brought me here from Pinsk in less than five minutes!"

"So you got here from Pinsk in less than five minutes," said Kolokov. "What good does that do you?"

"What good?" said Godunov. "It enables me to be the first in line to buy a pack of matches!"

Two Rumanian workers were walking along side by side. Their heads were bent low and their faces were sad and drawn. They were not talking to each other. Suddenly, one of the Rumanians spat on the ground and the other immediately did the same.

"That's enough," said one to the other. "If we continue, they'll think we're discussing politics."

A Russian Commissar was so discouraged with life in Moscow that he decided to commit suicide. One evening he walked out to the country, a loaf of bread tucked under his arm. When he came to a train junction, he laid down on the railroad tracks. A peasant passing by was amazed by the strange sight.

"What are you doing," he asked, "lying on these tracks?"

Said the commissar, "I'm going to commit suicide."

"What do you need the bread for?" asked the peasant.

The commissar answered, "In this country, by the time the train gets here, a man could starve to death."

Pravda has started a Letters-to-the-Editor column this month. It's a little different from the American version. They publish all beefs, complaints, and criticisms—but you have to give your name, address, and next of kin.

An amateur radio ham went delirious with excitement when he caught a newscast straight from Moscow on his set. "Our great athlete, Ivan Ivanovitch," the announcer was saying, "has just smashed all existing records for the 200-yard dash, the mile run, the five-mile run, and the 100-mile run, overcoming a blizzard, a range of mountains, and complete lack of water. Unfortunately, Ivanovitch's fantastic performance was in vain. He was captured and brought back to Russia.

A famous athlete, who had recently escaped from behind the Iron Curtain, was asked why the Russians excelled in marathon running.

He replied, "We use the border for the finish line."

Boris, who came from Russia, has been in this country only a few months. He did not speak English very well. One day he was asked, "Boris, what is it that you are most anxious to see in America?"

"Well," replied Boris, "I weesh most to meet the famous Mrs. Beech who have so many sons in the last war."

Red Riding Hood: A Russian condom

In Russia, the most popular game is "truth or consequences." You tell the truth or you go to Siberia.

"Suppose you were a Russian and the Kremlin announced that anyone could have a passport to go wherever he wanted, where would you go?"
"Up a tree."
"Up a tree! Why?"
"To avoid being trampled in the rush."

Petra Pavlova, the greatest ballerina of all Russia, was scheduled for her last performance.
"Petra," said Mischa, the manager, "you must give everything, everything."
That night, when the curtain opened, the spotlight found Petra poised on the first balcony. While the drums rolled, she sailed across the house, landed on the stage, in arabesque. She went into the wings and soon appeared on the second balcony. Again the drums, and she jumped to the stage and did a triple pirouette. Finally from the third balcony she landed in a perfect split. She didn't move. The audience was hysterical.
At last the curtain closed, the audience went home but Petra was motionless. Then the manager appeared.
"Mischa, do me a favor?" gasped Petra, still with legs asplit.
"Yes, Petra, anything."
"Mischa, rock me a little and break the suction."

SCANDINAVIAN

Swedish, Finnish, Danish, Norwegian

Olsen and his German friend, Schultz, went into a bar.

The bartender asked for their orders. "I tink," said Schultz, "I haf a leetle shin."

"What you tink of Schultz here?" said Olsen. "Ban in dis country saxteen year now and can't say yin yet!"

Did you hear about the Swedish wife who walked out on her husband?

She left his bed and smorgasbord.

Ole had reached the pier just as the ferry drew away, leaving a widening stretch of water.

"Yump, Ole, yump!" exclaimed Jens from the deck of the boat.

"Aye can't make it," replied Ole.

"Yump, Ole. Ya can make it in two yumps!"

A disheveled, beat-up Scandinavian was sitting in the gutter in front of a North Dakota saloon, laughing hilariously as the blood dripped from his nose.

"What's the joke?" asked a passerby.

"Aye bane in dar at da bar an' a faller come oop to me and hit me in da eye and say 'take dat, yu dam Norvegian!' An' hay poonch me on da nose and say 'Dat for yu, yu dam Novegian!' An' hay kick me into the street. Ha, ha!"

"But what's so funny about that?"

"Vy, aye bane Svede!"

Hedmann was driving 100 miles an hour when he was stopped by a motorcycle cop. "What's your hurry?" asked the officer.

"My brakes gave out," explained the Norwegian, "so I was trying to hurry home before I had an accident."

Norwegian Color TV: A keyhole into the next
apartment

Coffey was driving through Minnesota when his car broke down. Unable to find his monkey wrench, he went to the Johanson farm house. "Have you a monkey wrench here?" he asked the farmer.

"Naw," replied the Swede. "My brother bane got a cattle rench over there; my cousin got a sheep rench down there; but too cold for a monkey rench here."

Halvdon left Oslo and was met in New York at the pier by relatives. He proudly began showing off his

214

knowledge of the months of the year in English:
"Yoon, You-lie, All-guts, split timer, ox timber, no vonder, all vinter."

Did you hear about the girl working for the United Nations who hates the Danes and hates the Swedes— but would do anything for a Finn?

Who was the most famous Norwegian inventor?
Henry Fjord.

Sonja, a housemaid, at her friend's suggestion, decided to go out with the traveling salesman to make some extra money. Next day, her friend asked, "How did you make out?"

"I went out with him, like you said," replied Sonja, "and I did like he said. Then in the morning I said, 'Giff me ten dollar,' like you said. And he said, 'Go yump in the lake,' and when I come back he was gone!"

Olga, the Danish chambermaid at the Catskill mountain hotel was constantly being chased by Hirshberg, one of the guests. Every time he got near her, she ran away from him.

One day he grabbed the pretty Dane and whispered his sexual request in her ear. To his amazement, she agreed to meet him in his room that night. "If you're willing," said the Jewish man, "why did you keep running away from me?"

"Well," said the Danish girl, "all time I tink you vant extra towel!"

Soeltoft and Bergquist hired a row boat and were fishing on an inland lake. Suddenly, Soeltoft landed a big one. "This is some good spot to fish. How we gonna remember it?"

Bergquist immediately jumped overboard and disappeared beneath the surface. In a moment he climbed back on board. "What did you do?" asked Soeltoft.

"So we can remember this spot," said Bergquist, "I painted an 'X' on the bottom of the boat!"

"Boy, you are one stupid Norwegian!" shouted Soeltoft. "What we gonna do if next time we don't get the same boat!"

Swedish Girl: A smorgas broad

Did you hear about the Norwegian who went ice fishing?

He brought back fifty pounds of ice.

Mrs. Johnson's maid, Agneta, refused to be vaccinated on the grounds that she had been already.

"How many times?" asked Mrs. Johnson.

"Twice. Vunce in the kitchen and vunce in the garage."

"What doctor?"

"No doctor. Vas Mr. Yohnson."

Scarpelli picked up Birgitta at a bar and took her into a hallway to make love to her standing up. When he had finished he searched through his pockets to pay the girl and discovered, to his horror, that he had only a quarter.

The Italian felt bad because he didn't want to take advantage of the girl.

"Sorry, honey," said Scarpelli, "all I got is a quarter."

"Ay bane sorry, too," said the Swedish girl. "Ay bane got no change."

Olaf was on a convention in New York and, after having a few drinks at a fancy Madison Avenue cocktail lounge, the bartender handed him the check.

"New York is the most expensive place in the world," complained the Norwegian. "Back in Bismarck, North Dakota, you can drink as much as you want without paying, sleep in a fancy hotel for free, and wake up and find twenty dollars on your pillow."

"Come on, now," said the barkeep. "Has that ever happened to you?"

"No," admitted Olaf, "but it happens to my wife all the time."

Stockholm Dildo: An artificial Swedener

Stevenson got into the elevator of the coal mine chuckling to himself.

"What's the joke, Sven?" asked the foreman.

"Ay, got good yoke on Ole," said Norwegian miner. "Ay just find out Ole pay my wife five dollar just to foke her. And I foke her for nothing!"

Berquist hid in the closet when Frank, the husband of his girlfriend, returned unexpectedly. While hanging up his coat, Frank spotted the Swede's balls between two other garments. "What the hell are those?" he asked his wife.

"Eh, Christmas bells," she replied.

"Let's hear their peel," said the husband. He gave them a terrific whack with his fist.

A voice gasped, *"Yingle, yangle!* You sonava bitch!"

217

Swedish Massage: A Scandinavian workout

McIntyre and Svenson shared a cabin while working
their way across the ocean on a steamship, though they
worked different parts of the ship. The Irishman was a
deckhand, the Swede worked in the stoke-hold, wetting
down the fuel coke to prevent dangerous fumes.

When the ship docked and they were saying
goodbye, McIntyre asked, "Say, what the hell was it
you were doin' to work your way over?"

"Ay bane coke-soaker," said the Swede.

"Ye dirrty divil," said the Irishman, "and I nivir
suspected ye!"

Helga, the belle of cold Norway
Once hung by her heels in a doorway,
   She told her man Fred,
   "Get off of the bed,
I think I've just found one more way."

Inger and Hilda, two housemaids, were having their
pictures taken. The photographer stood behind his
camera to set the proper angle.

"Why is he looking at us like that?" asked Inger.

"He got to focus."

"No," said Inger. "You tell him yust to take the
picture first!"

A couple were applying for a marriage license.

"Your name?"

"Ole Olson."

"And yours?"

"Lena Olson."

"Any connection?"

The bride blushed. "Only vunce. He yumped me."

Both crews of the first two Viking longboats in the small bay sat ramrod-straight, oars held steady in an even line, while the men in the third vessel lolled wearily and dispiritedly over theirs, which dragged loosely.

"Sons of Odin," shouted the chief of the raiding party over the water, "yonder lies the undefended Saxon village! We here in the lead boat will loot! You men in the second boat will burn! And you men . . ."

"Oh, no," muttered an oarsman in the third longboat, "Don't tell me we're raping again!"

SCOTTISH

WHAT is the difference between a Scotsman and a coconut?

You can get a drink out of a coconut.

Scotchman: A guy who goes to a wedding with a broom
— and brings home the rice for dinner

"Excuse me, sir," said MacNabb, "but aren't you the gentleman that fetched my son out of the lake yesterday?"

"Why, yes, I am," said the embarrassed rescuer. "But that's all right—let's just say nothing more about it."

"Say nothing about it!" shrieked the Scot. "Indeed, mon, where's his cap?"

Scotty (hoping for free advice): Doctor, what should I
do for a sprained
ankle?
Doctor (also a Scot): Limp.

A frugal old female of Glasgow
Threw a ball which proved quite a fiasco
   At nine-thirty, about,
    The lights all went out . . .
Not for sex. She'd skipped paying the Gas Co.

A Scot, an Italian and a Jewish man were dining
together in an expensive restaurant. When the bill
arrived, the Scotsman promptly declared that he would
take it.
    The next day the newspaper carried a headline:
JEWISH VENTRILOQUIST SHOT IN RESTAURANT

Scotland Yard: 2' 11"

What is the difference between a Scotsman and a
canoe?
    A canoe tips.

Sergeant-Major MacGregor walked into a Glasgow
drugstore and took a beat-up condom out of his kilt.
"How much, mon," he asked the proprietor, "would it
cost to fix this?"
    "Let's see," murmured the druggist. "I could
launder and disinfect it, heat-weld the holes and tears
and insert a new elastic in the top. That would cost you
two shillings, the same as the price of a new one."
    MacGregor said that he would think it over.
    He returned the next day.
    "Ye've convinced me, mon," he announced. "The
regiment has decided to replace."

Jock: How do you like your radio, Mac?
Mac: Mon, it's grand, but the wee light's hard to read by.

Ferguson was out on his first date, and after taking his girl to a movie they went to a restaurant.

"Now don't go and eat yourself sick." he said, "just 'cause it ain't costing you nothin'."

A Mexican, an Italian, and a Scotsman were discussing what they would do if they awoke one morning to discover that they were millionaires.

The Mexican said he would build a bull ring.

The Italian said he would hire thirty hookers—one for each night of the month.

The Scotsman said he would go to sleep again and see if he could make another million.

McMasters, planning a trip to the Holy Land, was aghast when he found it would cost fifteen dollars an hour to rent a boat on the Sea of Galilee. "Mon," he said, "anywhere in Scotland it would be cheaper."

"Perhaps," said the travel agent, "but remember, the Sea of Galilee is the water on which our Lord walked."

"Oh, my," said the Scotsman, "it's nae wonder He walked."

Donaldson walked into MacAnally's house and found him trying to steam the wallpaper off the walls without tearing any of it.

"Why be so careful?" asked Donaldson. "You're just going to put up new paper, aren't you?"

"Like hell I am," said MacAnally. "I'm moving to another house and I'm trying to take the wallpaper with me."

It was a chip-in party—a reunion of old friends. The Englishman brought a cooked turkey; the Irishman brought a case of whiskey; the American brought a Virginia ham; and the Scotsman brought his brother.

Haggarty didn't have any tobacco for his pipe and he saw MacAndrews coming along.

"Might oi trouble ye fer the loan of a match?" asked the Irishman.

"Ay!" and the Scot gave him one.

"Faith, now!" exclaimed Haggarty. "If I haven't come out without any tobacco, and all the shops are shut."

"Ah!" said the Scot. "In that case ye'll no' be needin' that match."

A man on crutches hobbled up to MacDougal. "Please help me," he said, "I just lost my leg."

"I don't have time to help you look for it," said the Scot. "Why don't you put an ad in the papers?"

For a birthday gift, Ian's mother bought five yards of woolen plaid to make him his first kilt. But she only used three yards of the material.

When Ian's birthday came, he was delighted with it and his mother showed him how, by being thrifty, she had saved two yards of the material.

Ian was anxious to show the kilt to Laurie, his new girlfriend, but on the way to her house he stopped off to go swimming with the boys. When Ian dressed again, he put on his coat but, not being used to the kilt, he forgot it.

Ian hurried to Laurie's house, he rang the bell, and when she opened the door, he threw open his coat and said, "Look what I've got, Laurie, and there's two more yards of it at home!"

Stuart: Come on out for a while, Agnes, and we'll go for a walk.

Agnes: Nae, Stuart, I willna come ott wi' ye tonight.

Stuart: What's the matter, Agnes, dinna ye like the gleam in my eye?

Agnes: It isn't the gleam in your eye, Stuart, it's the tilt in your kilt.

After a Scottish Day parade in New York, a few of the paraders, still wearing their kilts, were having a few in the Loch Lomond Bar.

A girl approached the group of Scotties and said, "Hey, I've always wondered, but what do you really have under those kilts?"

Said MacBean, "I'm a mon of few words, lassie. Just gimme yer hand."

In Glasgow, every Sunday A.M., while the family was at church, Annie would be visited by her lover, Jock. One Sunday morning when the coast was clear, he started gaily whistling, "Annie Laurie."

· She gave him a disapproving look, and when he began to whistle another tune she hopped out of bed and began getting dressed.

"What's the matta?" asked Jock.

"I'll nae fornicate wi' a mon who whistles on the Sabbath!"

Andy: Do you know what MacNivin did with his first fifty-cent piece?

Tony: No.

Andy: Married her.

"I hear yer friend Tamson's married again."

"Aye, so he is. He's been a dear friend to me. He's cost me three wedding presents and two wreaths."

MacBain approached Currie and said, "I'm all upset. I can marry a wealthy widow who I don't love, or a poor lass that I love very much. What shall I do?"

"Weel, mon, I advise ye to listen to yer heart an' marry the lass ye love," said Currie.

"You're right! I will marry to the poor lass."

"In that case, kin ye give me the widow's address?" asked Currie.

A pretty lassie named McPherson
Was really the busiest person;
 Spent her days, for a fact,
 In the sexual act
And all of her nights in rehearsin'.

Did you hear about the Scotsman who was so stingy he slept with his mother-in-law, to save the "wear and tear" on his pretty bride?

MacLeod and his wife visited one of the circus airfields where they charge fifty dollars for a plane ride just around the town. Naturally, he wouldn't spend the money until the pilot approached him. "I'll take you and your wife up for nothing," he said, "It'll be a rough ride—but if you and your wife lets out one single word—one sound—while we're up there—then it's double."

MacLeod accepted the challenge and up they went. It really was a rough ride—dives—loops—turnovers. Finally they landed. "You win," said the pilot. "Not a word out of you."

"No," said the Scotsman, "but I almost did speak when my wife fell out."

"Well, Robert," said Donald, "and how do you like married life?"

"Not bad," replied Robert, "but she's always asking for money. Asking, asking all the time."

"And how much have you given her?"

"Oh, nothing yet."

The day after MacGregor's wife presented him with an offspring, the proud father was seen in a drugstore buying a baby bottle.

"Man, that's a scandalous extravagance," said a drinking buddy.

"It's necessary, though," sighed Mac, "the woman's gone and had triplets."

Angus, down from Aberdeen, was obviously enjoying his holiday in London. When he returned to his hotel each evening he was full of the wonders of the place.

Another guest, infected by Angus's delight asked him, "Is this your first time in London?"

"Aye, it is that," was the reply.

"You seem to be having such fun that I presume you haven't had a holiday for a considerable time," said the chatty gent.

"It's not only that," smiled Angus, "but it's my honeymoon as well."

"In that case," asked the guest, taken aback, "where is your wife?"

"Oh, she's been here before."

According to legend, Sir Harry Lauder, the famous Scots comedian, was leaving the stage door of the Alhambra Theatre in Glasgow when a woman rushed up to him, shaking a box in front of his face.

"Come on, Sir Harry," she beamed, "it's flag day — give till it hurts."

"Madam," he replied, "the very idea hurts."

The old couple had gone into an Edinburgh restaurant and ordered lamb chops. The waiter noticed that the woman hadn't touched hers.

"Something wrong, madam?" he inquired politely, "perhaps overdone?"

"No, no, laddie," she smiled, "I'm just waiting for my husband to finish. He's using the teeth first."

McClery visited his doctor for a checkup.

He carried with him a large amount of liquid specimen, which the M.D. examined in his laboratory.

"Everything's fine," announced the physician. "Couldn't find a thing wrong with your specimen."

"No sugar? No albumen?" asked McClery.

"None at all. You're okay."

"May I use your phone to call my wife?"

"Of course."

"Good news, dear," announced the Scot over the phone. "Neither you nor I nor the kids nor even Grandma Dougal have a thing the matter with us."

A New York newspaper received this letter from a reader named MacMillan:

"If you print any more jokes about Scotsmen, I shall discontinue borrowing your newspaper."

Mrs. McDermott looked out of the window as the family was going in to dinner, and wailed, "Och, Sandy, here comes company, I bet they haven't eaten yet."

"Quick!" shouted Mrs. McDermott, "Everybody out on the porch—with a toothpick!"

McCone made his wife keep a careful account of every penny she spent on herself, and once a week he examined it, to the accompaniment of groans of anguish and what-is-the-world-coming-to's. Once, going over the account he said, "Harriet! Harriet, do you think I'm made of money?"

"What's wrong, dear?" she asked.

"Wrong? You spent one dollar for corn plasters, fifty cents for aspirin and ten dollars to have your teeth pulled! That's eleven dollars and fifty cents you spent this week on your own personal pleasure!"

Feversham, an Englishman, went to a wedding service in Scotland and was most surprised when he noticed a collection plate being passed round.

"Is this a Scottish custom?" he whispered to the usher.

"Not usually," was the reply, "but on this occasion, the bride's father insisted."

Donald returned home to Scotland after being in America for thirty years. He wrote to his two brothers to meet him at the airport.

Two men with beards met him and he had difficulty recognizing his two brothers. "Why the beards?" he asked.

"Dinna ye remember, Donald? You took the razor with you."

STRANGER THAN FICTION
THE MAN WHO INVENTED SLOW MOTION
MOVIES GOT HIS IDEA WHILE WATCHING A
SCOTSMAN REACH FOR A RESTAURANT CHECK.

Wedding Guest: This is your fourth daughter to get married, isn't it?

McCavendish: Aye, and our confetti's gettin' awfully gritty.

"Father! Father!" shouted Kevin, rushing into the house, "coming from school, I ran home behind the bus all the way and saved fifty cents carfare."

"Spendthrift!" exclaimed his dad, slapping the boy in the face. "Why didn't you run home behind a taxicab and save three dollars and fifty cents?"

McCorkle, weary and dejected, sauntered up to the bar. "What's the trouble?" asked the bartender.

"It's yoorz," moaned the old timer. "I've got a terrible case of yoorz."

"What's yoorz?" asked the barkeep.

"A double Scotch, thanks," said the Scotsman.

What is so rare as a day in June?
Drinks on the house in a Scotch saloon.

A True Scot: A man who never sends his pajamas to the laundry unless he has a pair of socks stuck in the pocket

Kingsley had migrated all the way from Aberdeen to America and applied for a job in the police force. During his examination he was asked, "What would you do to disperse a crowd?"

"Well," replied the Scotsman, "I don't know what should be done in New York here, but I know what I'd do at home."

"What's that?"

"I'd pass round the hat."

What started the Grand Canyon?
A Scotsman lost a penny in a ditch.

Did you hear about the Scot who always went to fancy dress balls dressed as Napoleon — so that he could keep his hand on his wallet?

STINGIEST MAN IN SCOTLAND
HE LOOKS OVER THE TOP OF HIS GLASSES
FOR FEAR OF WEARING THEM OUT

McCarney was traveling from Omaha to Denver by train. He got into a furious argument with the conductor over his fare. The Scot accused the train man of trying to charge him too much and he refused to pay.

Finally, the conductor got disgusted. As the train passed over a bridge he picked up McCarney's suitcase and threw it out the window into the river below.

"You big bum!" screamed the Scotsman. "First you try to rob me and now you've drowned my son!"

Did you hear about the three Scotsmen who went to church one Sunday morning?

When the collection plate was handed round, one of them fainted and the other two carried him out.

"Your uncle was born in Scotland. I guess he's pretty stingy."

"Nah! He's not cheap. For my birthday he gave me a set of *Encyclopedia Britannica* — paperback."

Mrs. MacLord was dying and for three days her husband never left her bedside. Finally, he felt the need to visit his cronies down at the pub.

"Darlin'," he said, "I've got to go out for a wee bit. Now if you feel yourself dying, before you breathe your last breath, would you blow out the candle?"

Burns, MacDougall, and Ginsberg gathered at the casket of a dead friend. The first Scotsman turned to his companions and said:

"As you know I am a thrifty soul, but there is a legend in my family that if one places a wee bit of money in the casket to be buried with the body, it will ease the departed's way into the next world. For the sake of our friend, I place ten dollars in the casket with him."

The second Scot didn't want to look cheap, so he, too, took out a ten dollar bill and dropped it in the casket.

Then the Jewish man stepped forward. "You don't think I'm not gonna do my share, do you?" asked Ginsberg. He pulled out his checkbook and wrote a check for thirty dollars.

He placed it in the dead man's hand, and took the two ten dollar bills as change.

Did you hear about the Scotch weirdo who was so tight that he made all his obscene phone calls—collect?

Bobby was nervously clutching McCallion's hand as they marched into the fancy Hair Cutting Emporium.

"Just sit there and read the comics, son. I'll go first." And he flopped into the chair. "I'll have a shampoo," said the Scotsman, "then a haircut, a shave, a face massage, and a manicure."

An hour later, after a complete tonsorial job, McCallion stood up and said, "Just give the lad a good trim on the sides. I'm going next door for some cigarettes."

When the youngster finished getting his hair cut he went back to his reading. Time passed and soon the barber remarked, "My, but your father's been a way a long time."

"Oh, that's not my daddy," said the boy, "that's just a man who gave me a quarter if I'd come in and get my hair cut."

TURKISH

Two Turks met on the street. "Hello," said the first Turk. "Recognize me?"

"I can't remember your name, buddy, but the fez is familiar."

When the Sultan entered his harem unexpectedly, his wives let out a terrified sheik.

The Sultan got sore at his harem,
And invented a scheme for to scare 'em
　　He caught him a mouse
　　Which he loosed in the house
The confusion is called harem-scarem!

Crandall had worked and traveled all over the world. "For awhile I held the post of the chief spitter in the Sultan's harem," he told a friend.

"What in the world is a chief spitter?"

"All I had to do," explained Crandall, "was to spit on each of the Sultan's wives; when one sizzled, I would take her to the Sultan."

A Sultan whose loves grew so vastly
Just couldn't love any steadfastly.
　　Someone asked him in fun
　　If he'd slept twice with one.
He replied, "Such a thought is most ghastly."

Mrs. Rubenstein returned to the Bronx after a visit to Turkey and began telling her neighbor about it. "They must have a girls' ball team in the Sultan's harem," she said.

"Why's that?"

"I overheard one of the girls ask the Sultan if she was in tomorrow's line-up."

The Sultan had nine wives. Eight of them had it pretty soft.

The ladies of the harem were seated in a circle, casting dice on a gorgeous Persian rug. Around the circle went the cubes in the hands of the excited players.

"It's Zenobia tonight!" they screamed in unison. "Poor Zenobia!"

With a deep sigh Zenobia arose and with dragging steps passed through the velvet portierers.

"I'd hate to be that poor kid!" remarked the wife called Little Turkey. "That's the third time this week she's had to wash the dishes!"

In the harem, a lonely girl calls
But the guard, all-unheeding, just sprawls.
   When he's asked if he cheats
   On the sultan, he bleats
"Oh, I would—but I ain't got the balls!"

The Sultan called for his eunuch. "I am in the mood," he said. "Bring me wife number two hundred twenty-eight."

So the eunuch ran out of the palace and into the harem. He ran through the garden, past the orchard, and up the steps. And he soon returned with wife number 228.

A little later, the Sultan sent for his eunuch again. "I want more! Go get wife number thirty-six!"

The eunuch ran through the palace, to the harem, through the garden, the orchard, and then up the steps. He brought back wife number 36.

Then the Sultan asked for wife number 74. Again the eunuch raced to the harem. When he returned with wife number 74 he was panting heavily. Then he suddenly collapsed and died on the spot.

Moral: It's not the women in your life that can kill you— it's the chasing after them.